DON'T OFFER PAPAYA
101 Tips for Your First Time
Around the World

Atlas & Boots

CONTENTS

Foreword i

Introduction iii

Chapter 1: Planning 1

Chapter 2: Documentation 10

Chapter 3: Packing 18

Chapter 4: Budgeting 30

Chapter 5: Getting Around 37

Chapter 6: Accommodation 47

Chapter 7: Outdoor 52

Chapter 8: Culture Shock 63

Chapter 9: Wellbeing 71

Chapter 10: Health 79

Chapter 11: Photography 91

Chapter 12: Language 99

Chapter 13: Safety & Security 113

Chapter 14: Working On The Road 122

Chapter 15: Coming Home 128

Appendix A: Packing List 134

Appendix B: Apps & Sites 138

FOREWORD: DON'T OFFER PAPAYA

Hernán Echavarría
Local Guide, Real City Tours
Medellín, Colombia

I first met Kia and Peter on a Friday afternoon in Medellín, Colombia, just as the day's heat was settling in and making everyone feel a little loose and crazy.

They had booked onto Real City Tours' free walking tour of Medellín and had fortuitously landed in my group. Straight away I could tell that Peter, the son of a history teacher, was intrigued by my city and indeed my country.

Medellín, once a city of two halves, is now healing at the rifts. What was once seen as a dark and dangerous city full of drugs and crime and poverty has become a monument to progress. Medellín is loud and discordant and yet sweet and sophisticated. It teems with modern conveniences yet dazzles with history around every street corner. It is a relic of what has passed and a sign of things to come.

Kia and Peter saw both faces of Medellín, but not without a warning first.

There are two rules on the streets of Colombia, I told them as I tell you now. First, don't offer papaya. Second, if papaya is offered, someone has to take it.

'Papaya' in this case is a byword for your valuables. If you leave your bag slung over the back of your chair, you're offering papaya. If you leave your camera on a restaurant table, you're offering papaya. If you walk down a dark and deserted alley, you're offering papaya. You don't need to be on red alert at every second of the day, but you do need to be mindful of your behaviour and your belongings.

Colombia is changing and every person that visits our country is part of the changing of the story. Kia and Peter and others like them come and see the country for what it is. They share its tales and triumphs and encourage others to experience the same.

So, no, don't offer papaya but do go out and see the world. Meet eccentric locals, see extraordinary landscapes, fight pre-judgments, talk to strangers, learn to dance and, of course, come to Colombia along the way. I'll be waiting.

- Hernán

INTRODUCTION

In August 2014, we – Kia Abdullah and Peter Watson – quit our jobs in publishing and teaching and left the concrete streets of London for our first trip around the world.

With years of exploring already behind us, we thought we knew everything there was to know about long-term travel. Yet, somehow, we still offered papaya in Colombia, got a funny tummy in Tonga, fell off a bike in Bora Bora and broke down in Bolivia (in more ways than one).

Fast forward two years and we're far more wise and a little less cocky. We learnt a great deal from our time abroad, from psychological tricks to practical tips for making the most of life on the road.

We've gathered our best advice – read by 100,000 people every month at atlasandboots.com – and created this guide to help travellers both experienced and new prepare for their first trip around the world.

Personal anecdotes mixed with succinct travel advice tell you everything you need to know, from mind-hacking taxi drivers into accepting your fare to the number one rule for not looking like a douche.

We don't think you need a 300-page tome on how to travel – part of the joy is figuring it out yourself – but a streamlined guide will definitely be of use. So keep this book on you, glance through it on your long commute and use it to plan, book and enjoy your extraordinary trip around the world.

We'll see you out there!

Atlas & Boots
atlasandboots.com

Kia and Peter diving in Tonga, 2014

CHAPTER 1: PLANNING

1. Use the budget formula

Here is the formula we used to calculate the budget for our first time around the world. All prices here and throughout the book are presented in US dollars ($).

- Total Budget = (No. of Months x $2,000) + $600
- Daily Budget = (Total Budget x 0.75) / No. of Days
- Big-Ticket Items = Total Budget x 0.25

We needed $600 for travel insurance and vaccinations, the latter of which cost a painful $400.

We reserved 25% of our budget for big-ticket items (flights and multi-day treks) and used 75% for daily expenditure (food, accommodation, day-to-day transport). We struggled towards the end but that was partly because we were cavalier with our budget at the beginning. If you stick to your daily budget, the formula should work as a good benchmark.

Some hardened backpackers will scoff at the above and insist that they crossed Southeast Asia on $10 a day, but we didn't want to be uncomfortable. We booked a private room for all but 10 nights during our yearlong trip and had a private bathroom about 80% of the time. If you're happy staying in dorms, then shave 10% off your total budget.

2. Solo or no?

There's a certain wildness and romance in travelling alone but it does have its drawbacks too. Here's what to consider when making your decision.

The pros of solo travel

Forces you to make friends: If you're not proactive about making friends, you face the prospect of spending your entire trip alone which is just no fun. Travelling alone forces you from your shell and encourages others to approach you too.

Builds your confidence: As you are entirely in charge of the trip logistics, you have to talk to lots of different people. Over the course of a long trip, your confidence will bloom.

Offers complete freedom: Solo travel allows you to set your own pace and control your own schedule. You can indulge in your interests without worrying about boring a companion. Conversely, you don't have to go on a three-hour tour of a transport museum if you're not so inclined.

Speeds up language learning: Travelling alone means you will likely interact more with locals. The more you talk to them, the more you'll improve your vocabulary.

The cons of solo travel

Loneliness: You won't have a dining companion by default, or someone with whom to share your trip highs and lows. After a long stretch of time, this can lead to a sense of loneliness.

Stress: It was a girl called Alice in Quito who said 'sometimes, I just want to cry' in describing the exhaustion of organising everything herself. Whether it's having to lug your backpack into the toilet with you because there's no one else to watch it, or trying to decipher what on earth happened to the bus that's three hours late, having sole responsibility can make solo travellers more stressed than their buddied-up peers.

Expense: From paying a single supplement fee for rooms and tours, to shouldering the cost of every taxi alone, travelling solo can be more expensive.

Less safe: Travelling with a companion means you always have someone watching your back. Solo travel can be less safe if you're not diligent about informing friends and family of your whereabouts.

Do you want the romance of venturing alone to the great unknown, or do you want a safety net? Only you can make that decision.

3. RTW or plan as you go?

A round-the-world ticket (RTW) has several pros and cons.

The pros of RTW

It may be cheaper: Depending on your mileage, route and number of stops, RTW can cost between $2,000 to $10,000, possibly less if you limit yourself to a basic three-stop route.

Less stress on the road: With RTW, you know for certain that you can get from A to B because it's booked in and confirmed; most of the planning stress is done upfront. In Samoa, we booked our flights to Tonga at a beach fale using a sketchy internet connection via dongle while charging our laptop with pay-as-you-go electricity. An RTW ticket alleviates this stress.

Allows better budgeting: Your trip has a start date and end date, so you know exactly how many days you need to budget for. With plan as you go, your budget fluctuations are much wilder because flights have to be absorbed by your day-to-day budget.

Collects air miles: Sticking with one group of airlines means you can fairly easily build up your air miles. It's not unusual to build up enough for a long-haul flight.

The cons of RTW

Lack of spontaneity: If we had chosen RTW, we wouldn't have spent a month in Tahiti, taken a last-minute 16-day cruise across the Pacific, summited the world's tallest (not highest) mountain or taken an impromptu road trip across four states in America. Plan as you go allows you to change your plan without repercussions.

It's complicated: Not only are you limited by mileage and number of stops, you will also be limited by a number of additional rules. Examples include: you must cross both the Pacific and Atlantic oceans, you can stop in a city only once but can transit it up to three times, you can stop in a continent a restricted number of times, you must start and end in the same country, you must travel in one direction, your overland travel may count towards your mileage limit even though you're not flying and so on.

Follows the tourist trail: If your RTW ticket is both cheap and easy, it's likely that you'll be following scores of other backpackers around the world. If you're doing London, Bangkok, Singapore, Sydney, LA, New York, London for example, chances are so will thousands of others.

Actually, it may *not* be cheaper: Most RTW tickets don't include the big budget airlines and if you're travelling an unusual route, you may have to cough up for additional flights in between destinations. RTW also precludes the possibility of finding super-cheap modes of transport which are far easier to root out when you're actually in a country or region (e.g. cargo ships, trains, hitch hiking etc).

Which one?

At Atlas & Boots, we prefer to plan as we go. There's a freedom in not knowing where we're going beyond the next few weeks. It leaves open the possibility of jumping on a boat, taking a last-minute road trip or settling somewhere for a while if the idea strikes. For us, it's the most interesting way to travel.

4. Quit your job or take a sabbatical?

If you have been working at a company for some years, you may be able to take a sabbatical. In some cases, this is offered in the standard employment contract. In others, you will have to make a special case.

Quitting offers the ultimate flexibility. If you want to extend your time away by six months like we did, you have the freedom to do so. If you want to settle in Samoa, you can. On the flipside, quitting leaves you in a more vulnerable situation financially as you won't have a job waiting for you on return.

Taking a sabbatical on the other hand offers less flexibility (you have to be back on a specific date) but it does offer more security. You will have a job waiting for you on return, so you know exactly where you stand.

At Atlas & Boots, we chose to go take the leap and quit. It was right for us because we knew we wanted not just a career break, but a career change. We didn't want to go back to our old jobs and our old lives when we returned. For us, the decision was easy.

5. Plan your seasons

Some of our best advice was gleaned from getting it wrong. This is one of those occasions.

In May 2015, we were racing through Chile trying to get to Patagonia before it shut down for winter. Traditional wisdom (guidebooks, forums) told us that while it wasn't ideal to visit the area in May, it *was* possible. Unfortunately, due to the relentless fog, we saw nothing of Torres del Paine, Cerro Torre or Fitz Roy, some of the most dramatic mountains in Patagonia. Perhaps this was just bad luck as other visitors in the area did manage to see some sights, but in hindsight we shouldn't have visited out of season. Shoulder seasons have always worked well for us (lower prices, fewer tourists) but out of season was a step too far.

On a trip around the world, you won't be able to see everything at its optimum time but as a general rule, avoid visiting out of season, especially when the sights are dependent on weather.

6. Think about your goals

Before planning your trip around the world, consider what it is you want to gain. Are you travelling out of pure curiosity about the world, or do you want to change your life? Perhaps you want to learn a language, change careers or find somewhere to settle.

If you have a tangible goal, start planning for it early. For example, if you want to learn Spanish, you can plan a one-month stop in Mendoza, Argentina, to study at a language school instead of muddling through on the road. Perhaps your thing is Scuba diving, mountain climbing or visiting UNESCO world heritage sites. Considering your goals beforehand can elevate your experience from a round-the-world jolly to a life-changing journey. You may never have a stretch of time like this again so use it wisely.

Our goal: We wanted to visit places we might never see again. We chose the South Pacific because it was literally on the other side of the world. We knew that most people don't get to take individual vacations to Fiji, Tonga and Samoa so we made sure we saw those places when we had the chance. Who knows if we'll ever be in the South Pacific again? Likewise, when we were in South America we made sure we visited Easter Island and the Galápagos.

7. Prepare your credit rating

Your credit rating is important for two reasons. Firstly, it will determine whether or not you can secure a good travel credit card. Prime options like the Halifax Clarity Card won't charge you cash withdrawal fees, saving you a substantial amount of money (e.g. $600 on a $20,000 budget!). These prime options require a very strong rating so start improving yours as early as possible: moneysavingexpert.com/loans/credit-rating-credit-score.

Secondly, your credit rating may be affected if you travel long term with no permanent address. Make sure you register to vote by proxy and have your bills and bank statements going to one address to keep your financial records as tidy as possible.

8. Get fit

If you're planning a trip around the world, chances are you have a few items on your list that require a level of fitness (e.g. trekking Machu Picchu, climbing Kilimanjaro, tackling a volcano or two). Consider these in advance and think about how fit you need to be.

It was in 'Travels' that author Michael Crichton admitted

to tackling Kili while woefully underprepared. He underestimated the level of fitness required and ended up blistered, exhausted and a burden on his companions.

Our advice is to work on your fitness as early as possible to give yourself the best chance of enjoying not only demanding activities but everyday travelling too. Walking long distances and carrying your backpack will be less taxing if you're fit.

9. Don't be snobby about guidebooks

In much of the travel press, 'not in the guidebook' has become a lazy shortcut for denoting authenticity. Articles and blogs make pejorative references to 'guidebook-toting' tourists and, for many travellers, travelling without a guide has become a badge of honour.

The truth is, travel guidebooks are invaluable resources when you're in a new country. Naturally, there will be some 'sheep' who are all having the same banana milkshake at the same roadside cafe because page 207 in their guide to Thailand told them to do it, but that doesn't mean everyone with a travel guidebook is a conformist and a bore.

Guidebooks offer more information than the travel press and provide more knowledge than other travellers (and even some locals). Guidebooks can save you money and provide wider context to new destinations. Don't be snobby about taking one along. We have always used Lonely Planet (shop.lonelyplanet.com)

10. Don't worry – it's not as hard as you think

Prior to leaving, I (Kia) was worried about how I would adjust to life on the road. Unlike Peter, I am a planner. I like to know how things will pan out and I appreciate my creature comforts. As such, I worried that I would be overwhelmed or fatigued or bored by life on the road.

In reality, it was far easier than expected. *All* of it was easier: the saving up, the quitting of jobs, the planning and the packing, the farewells, the 32-hour bus journeys, the delays, the cockroaches and even the bittersweet end.

Our trip showed us the true meaning of freedom and we still believe, unequivocally and undoubtedly, that it was the best decision we ever made.

CHAPTER 2: DOCUMENTATION

11. Check your passport

Let's start with the basics. First, make sure your passport will be valid for the entire duration of your trip and six months beyond its conclusion. Many countries require six months' validity on your passport before granting you entrance, so make sure you have this covered.

Second, make sure you have enough blank pages to accommodate all the stamps and visas you may acquire. Some countries don't require visas or blank pages for stamps, but it's wise to assume that if you will be visiting 10 countries, you will need 10 blank pages in your passport.

Depending on your nationality, ordering a passport can be expensive and lengthy, so factor this into your budget and planning.

The same advice applies to your driver's licence or equivalent ID. It's unwise to carry around your passport when out and about, so a secondary form of reliable ID like a driver's licence is useful to have with you at all times. If your licence has expired or has a photo of you from 10 years ago in that embarrassing grunge stage, then it's essentially useless so make sure it's up to date. A driver's licence will also come in use at the embassy if you were to lose your passport. If that happens, see tip 88. What to do in an emergency.

12. Buy annual travel insurance

In January 2014, British adrenaline junkie Ben Cornick jumped out of a plane in Fiji at 12,000 feet. There was no way to know at the moment he leapt out of the aircraft that his parachute would fail and that he would plummet to Earth, breaking his leg in three places and shattering his elbow.

It gets worse: Ben hadn't bought travel insurance and had to pay £20,000 upfront for treatment to save his leg. His parents pulled together their life savings and readied to sell their house. But then there was an unlikely twist: following media coverage of Ben's predicament, complete strangers donated money to pay his medical bills, massively reducing the cost to his parents. Thankfully, this case has a happy ending but clearly we wouldn't all be so lucky.

The purpose of this story isn't to scaremonger; it's to illustrate that accidents can happen even if, like Ben and skydiving, you have done something a thousand times with no injury. The answer to 'should I get travel insurance?' is yes – doubly so if you're going on a long-term trip.

You may have an annual travel insurance policy as part of your current bank account or another benefit, but be aware that this likely covers a year's worth of separate trips, usually up to a maximum of 30 days. For a long-term trip, you need long-term insurance. We use World Nomads (worldnomads.com).

Make a note of the insurance company's emergency phone number as well as your policy number in your phone, in email and in a notebook so that you always have access to it.

13. Secure your visas

Depending on your destination, you may have to apply for visas before you leave your home country. These can take several weeks to process and often have to be issued within a specific timeframe. Each country has its own set of agreements with others, as well as fluctuating fees, so do your research before you leave.

Websites like Visa HQ (visahq.com) can process visas for you but we tend to go directly to the relevant government website to avoid the many scams online.

When applying, make sure you select the correct type of visa. If you're planning to work or volunteer in the country, you may need a working or business visa instead of a tourist visa. Again, research is key.

Finally, make sure your visa covers your entire stay. Extending visas can be a bureaucratic nightmare, especially if you've accidentally overstayed in which case you could face a heavy fine.

14. Document your jabs

When I (Peter) first started travelling over 10 years ago, I had a whole heap of vaccinations. I can't remember exactly how many, but it was enough to warrant the issue of a little yellow booklet containing a list of treatments and dates. The reason I can't remember the list of jabs is because I promptly lost the little yellow booklet and all the information within.

When it came to our trip around the world several years later, we had vaccinations against all sorts of potentially harmful diseases including rabies, hepatitis and yellow fever.

"I swear I've had some of these before," I pondered to myself...

After returning from our trip around the world, while unpacking our stored belongings, I discovered the little yellow booklet that was first issued nearly 10 years ago, confirming that I had indeed been vaccinated multiple times

against the same diseases, wasting money, time and med
resources.

I have now made copies of all my vaccination details and
saved them digitally. We strongly advise that you do the
same.

15. Prepare onward tickets

Some countries need to check that you have an onward
ticket not only for their country but the next one too. For
example, let's say you have been in Fiji for a week and are
now leaving for Samoa. Before Fijian authorities let you
board the flight to Samoa, they need to check that you have
an onward ticket from Samoa. This ensures you will depart
even if you run out of money. Without an onward ticket, you
could be refused entry.

The obvious option is to purchase an onward flight, train
or bus ticket but this can be more expensive than a last-
minute option. It can also impede your flexibility as you have
to stick to rigid transport plans or risk losing money on
unused tickets. Even if you purchase fully refundable tickets,
the bureaucracy of refunding those tickets can be
burdensome.

There are alternative options available. Websites like
onwardflights.com and flyonward.com offer to "rent" you
onward tickets for a nominal sum of a few dollars. We
haven't tried these services but they claim to be completely
legal and are certainly a cheaper option than buying
refundable tickets.

Another option is to "manufacture" an onward ticket.
Now, we at Atlas & Boots certainly don't condone this type
of nefarious activity but if we *did*, we may or may not have
done something similar in the past. Some basic Photoshop
skills are enough to adapt an old e-ticket with upcoming
flight details. We can't guarantee this will work and it will
always depend on the airline and the country's border
officials, but it may or may not have proved consistently

the past. The safest and most secure
to just buy onward tickets (refundable or
ngs of this nature, do your research

16. Carry photocopies

Make digital copies of the following documents and store
them on your smartphone, your laptop and in a secure
location online (we use Google Drive).

- Passport and other ID
- Travel insurance
- Visas
- Documentation of your jabs
- Onward tickets

It's worth making physical photocopies of your passport, ID
and travel insurance too. Your passport is most likely to be
lost or stolen if you carry it unnecessarily. It can be dropped
or misplaced while you forage around in your bag or, worse,
stolen when you're out and about. Carrying a photocopy
avoids this risk.

When we travel, we carry copies of our passports in our
daypacks as well as spares in our main luggage. If you need
to show identification to officials, a photocopy will usually
suffice, especially coupled with a driver's licence or similar
ID.

17. Prepare a will

It's a bit morbid we know but writing a will is worth
considering if you're planning an extended trip around the
world.

Travelling in most parts is just as safe as, say, living in
London but it's sensible to plan for the worst. Without a

will, a person's estate is divided up according to the law, which may not reflect their wishes. Write a will to protect your loved ones. This can be done via a solicitor or will-writing specialist. You can even do it yourself if the division of estate is straightforward. See moneysavingexpert.com/family/free-cheap-wills for more information.

18. Create a password sheet

Modern life involves so many disparate accounts, it's not unusual to forget specific details amid the mass of usernames, passwords, security questions, passcodes and so on.

If you need to access one of your accounts on the road, you don't want to be digging through email to try and locate the details or, worse, calling home to ask someone to sift through boxed paperwork. As such, make sure you have a record of your access details.

Tools like LastPass (lastpass.com) will save passwords for you, but some banks will prevent this type of storage. As such, you may wish to use a Google Sheet to record your details but encode your answers so that you will understand what they mean, but a wayward hacker would not. For example, if your password is 'ToroRosso1984', perhaps TR would act as enough of a prompt. In this way, you can easily access accounts associated with your bank, credit card, mobile phone, tax, mortgage, service charge, ground rent, Apple ID and so on.

In the sheet, make sure you record the relevant companies' customer service numbers, contact emails and complaints procedures in case you need to contact them on the road. It's also worth including a set of embassy numbers.

Naturally, this is a terrible idea if you have easily crackable passwords and are prone to leaving your email logged in on public machines. If that is the case, then disregard everything we've said and just wing it.

19. Create a checklist

Create a checklist of everything you need to do before you
leave. We suggest the following.

6 months to go
Update passport if applicable
Update driver's licence if applicable
Start learning the language
Prepare a will

3 months to go
Get a travel credit card
Book outbound flight
Complete home repairs (test smoke alarm, copy keys)
Get an EHIC card if applicable

2 months to go
Book vaccinations
Visit dentist
Visit doctor
Stock up on medicine
Buy travel insurance
Find tenants if applicable
Secure visas
Sell or dump unwanted possessions

1 month to go
Hand in your notice
Inform HMRC or your equivalent tax body
Inform utility companies of departure date
Change address (bank, mobile phone, property)
Set up mail forwarding service
Buy items on our packing list (see Appendix A: Packing List)
Download apps (see Appendix B: Apps & Sites)
Create hard and digital copies of documentation
Create password sheet

1 week to go

Back up all your phone data
Install Find My iPhone or relevant security software
Print flight tickets
Prepare and print onward ticket
Pack everything
Leave cheques with a trusted family member for any upcoming payments
Clean apartment or house
Put items into storage
Change money
Say goodbyes

1 day to go

Give final utility meter readings
Leave keys with agent

CHAPTER 3: PACKING

20. How to choose the right backpack

For a trip around the world, we recommend travelling with a backpack as opposed to a suitcase or duffel bag. A backpack is more versatile and easier to handle, especially over different terrains and road surfaces. Try rolling a suitcase over pot-holed dirt tracks in Tanzania!

For long-term travel, a backpack around the 45- to 70-litre mark will be sufficient, depending on your size.

How to fit a backpack

This is the most important aspect of choosing a backpack. Get it right and you'll have a pack that is comfortable, supportive and stable in all conditions. Get it wrong and you'll almost certainly suffer from shoulder, hip and back pain.

Don't order your backpack online without trying it on first. Visit a physical store and test different packs to find one that fits.

The right backpack should be fitted according to your torso length and waist size.

Torso length: Backpacks are usually available in different sizes, from extra-small to large. These vary by manufacturer so try on your backpack to ensure it's not too tall or too short for your torso. Some backpacks have an adjustable suspension which can be tweaked to fit your torso –

especially useful if you're between sizes. The downside is that an adjustable suspension adds a little bit of weight to the backpack.

Waist size: Most of a backpack's weight – 80% or more – should be supported by your hips. It's a myth that your shoulders and back take the weight. It's therefore essential that your backpack fits your hips snugly and rests on them comfortably without being too tight. Backpack hip belts usually accommodate a wide range of hip sizes. People with narrow waists occasionally find they cannot make a standard hip belt tight enough and need a smaller size. Some packs offer interchangeable hip belts, making it possible to swap one size for another.

Women's backpacks: Because women have smaller frame sizes, brands usually design backpacks for them separately. A woman's torso dimensions are generally shorter and narrower than a man's. Likewise, hip belts and shoulder straps are contoured for increased comfort with the female form in mind.

Features of a backpack

Your needs will likely differ depending on a number of things: the equipment you carry, your range of activities, your level of strength and the terrain you'll be covering. For example, a hiker may pack walking poles while most round-the-world travellers would not.

WALKING POLE /
ICE AXE LOOPS

ZIPPED FRONT
PANEL

LID

COMPRESSION
STRAPS

ROLL MAT /
ACCESSORY
STRAPS

STRETCH
SIDE POCKETS

FRONT
STASH
POCKET

LOAD LIFTERS

SHOULDER
STRAPS

CHEST
STRAP

BACK PANEL

HIP BELT
POCKET

HIP BELT

SLEEPING BAG COMPARTMENT

Below is a list of features to look out for, divided into essential features and optional ones.

Essential features

Hip belt: A hip belt that fits correctly can make for a great hiking experience. Conversely, it can make for a miserable experience if it doesn't fit well. The pack's weight should be distributed evenly so it doesn't leave your shoulders aching. Usually, the bigger the pack the beefier the padding, offering maximum support and comfort when carrying heavier loads

Shoulder straps: As with the hip belts, the thickness and type of padding used on the shoulder straps will change with the size of the pack. Thick padded straps provide comfort and support while thinner ones offer better flexibility. Mesh straps provide better ventilation.

Load lifters: These adjustment straps may look small but they are essential to carrying loads as comfortably as possible. They connect the shoulder straps to the top of the pack frame and can be used to change the angle and distance of the pack in relation to your body. This helps prevent a heavy pack from pulling away from you and keeps the weight of your pack centred on your hips.

Chest strap: The chest strap (or sternum strap) is attached to the shoulder straps and when fastened sits across the chest. Both the position and the length of the strap should be adjustable. This will improve the stability of the pack and keep shoulder straps stable by stopping them slipping.

Back panel: This should be contoured and padded for comfort. It should also be adjustable and include foam channels to provide cushioning that also improves breathability. For warm weather hiking you may consider a pack with a suspended mesh system which offers better ventilation.

Optional features

Lid: The lid usually incorporates a pocket for easy-access storage at the top of your pack. In some cases the lid can also be removed to save weight or even to use as a small hip pack.

Zipped front panel: This can be unzipped for easy access to the main compartment (sometimes called front loading compartments). We highly recommend buying a backpack with this feature.

Front stash pocket: Great in changeable weather. Perfect for stashing your jacket, guidebook, camera, rain cover etc.

Stretch side pockets: Usually for storing water bottles, often made from a stretch material for an easy and secure fit.

Sleeping bag (or lower) compartment: Two compartments make organisation easier. Commonly used to store a sleeping bag, the base compartment is usually separated from the main pack by an internal, sometimes adjustable, divider. It's also a good place to store dirty laundry or muddy shoes!

Compression straps: Use these straps to reduce the volume of your pack. They're particularly useful if your pack isn't full, as they'll help keep the load stable.

Hip belt pockets: Quick-access pockets are great for snacks, phones, wallets, gloves and other small essentials.

Roll mat/accessory straps: Often used to secure a roll mat, these can also act as general lash points, particularly useful for storing a tent.

Walking pole/ice axe loops: Use these loops for your walking poles and/or ice axes.

21. Compartmentalise your backpack

"Okay, I finally admit it. I am indeed a Nerdlinger," I wrote to my old desk-mate with a copy of the below.

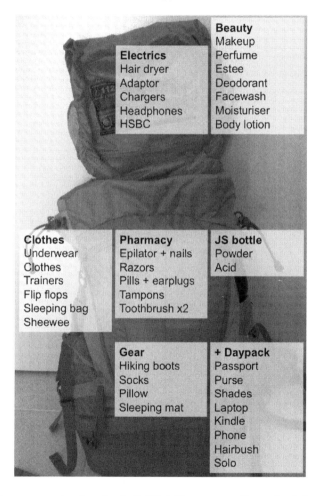

Electrics	Beauty
Hair dryer	Makeup
Adaptor	Perfume
Chargers	Estee
Headphones	Deodorant
HSBC	Facewash
	Moisturiser
	Body lotion

Clothes	Pharmacy	JS bottle
Underwear	Epilator + nails	Powder
Clothes	Razors	Acid
Trainers	Pills + earplugs	
Flip flops	Tampons	
Sleeping bag	Toothbrush x2	
Sheewee		

Gear	+ Daypack
Hiking boots	Passport
Socks	Purse
Pillow	Shades
Sleeping mat	Laptop
	Kindle
	Phone
	Hairbush
	Solo

As an organisation freak, I (Kia) like punctuality, schedules and order. Under normal circumstances, I unpack and organise everything as soon as I reach a new destination.

When constantly on the move, however, unpacking everything just isn't practical; you have to learn to live out of a backpack. And therein lies the problem.

On the road, I found myself constantly hunting for one thing or another until, eventually, much to Peter's amusement, I decided to name parts of my backpack and list what each contained. Following this, whenever I packed or unpacked, I made sure I put things in their correct place making it far, far easier to find, use and store things. You don't have to go as far as creating a diagram like me, but a loose designation will definitely help.

22. Travel light... no, lighter

In some ways, overpacking is a rite of passage: you have to do it to learn how not to do it. Of course, there is an easier way. By gleaning advice from other travellers and being strict with yourself, packing light is perfectly possible. Here's where to start.

Buy a bag that seems too small: Parkinson's law states that "work expands so as to fill the time available for its completion". In a similar vein, your toiletries and 'must-have' knick knacks will expand to fill the space available. To combat this, buy a bag that seems too small. This brute-force tactic will help by forcing you to select what you really need versus what you think you need.

Limit clothing to one third of your bag: Take only what you need for one week and wash as you go. To get more out of your clothes, make sure your items complement each other so you can create 'new' outfits on the go. Shell out for lightweight clothing and layer up instead of taking bulky jumpers. It's also worth trying packing cubes to keep your clothes organised and compressed.

Pack for the best-case scenario: So many of us overpack because we want to cover all eventualities. *What if I need more socks in Peru? What if I can't buy tampons in Rio? What if our phone charger breaks in Bolivia?* Instead of worrying about the worst, pack for the best-case scenario and simply buy yourself out of tricky situations. Even in remote places like Tanna Island in Vanuatu or Mafana Island in Tonga, we were able to buy what we needed in bigger towns close by. Don't take a year's supply or a 'just in case' backup of anything.

Ask yourself 'will I use this every week?' When considering an item, ask yourself if you will use it every week. If the answer is no, leave it at home. You can make an exception for big-ticket items like sleeping bags if you'll be camping a lot, or a mosquito net if you're in malarial areas but in most cases, if you won't use it every week, don't pack it. Equally, don't get attached to low-value items. Peter refused to throw away our relatively cheap snorkel mask after the South Pacific, so he carried it for five months in South America. We used it twice (when we could have hired instead). Don't make the same mistake.

Let yourself go: Every time I teased Peter about the aforementioned snorkel mask, he gleefully reminded me that I was lugging around a glass bottle full of Angel perfume which I'll admit now was completely unnecessary. I also packed two types of cleanser and three types of bras (normal, bandeau, sports). On the road, few people will notice or care what you look like, so leave the luxuries at home. Don't worry about frizzy hair (leave your straighteners at home), don't worry about bra straps showing beneath your halterneck, don't worry about smelling like a delicate blend of sweet red fruits, soft caramel, honey and praline combined with the captivating power of Patchouli and vanilla. It's really not that important.

Pack multi-purpose products: Where possible, pack products that work doubly hard. From multi-purpose soaps to universal travel adaptors, these will help immensely in packing light.

Buy solid versions of toiletries: Liquids are disproportionately heavy. Instead of packing big bottles of shampoo and other toiletries, opt for solid versions. These will be lighter, smaller, more durable, less messy and longer lasting.

Streamline your shoes: This is tricky if you're going on a long-term trip covering a wide variety of situations. Peter packed flip-flops, hiking boots and smart(ish) trainers, the last of which he wore in formal settings. I packed flip-flops, ballet flats, hiking boots and sports sandals. To be honest, I used them all regularly and am glad I packed them – but four pairs of footwear are the absolute maximum.

Streamline your leisure gadgets: We packed a wide variety of gadgets including phones, cameras, Kindles and laptops. We were working on the road so needed our laptops but could have left behind a number of the other items. Your phone can act as a camera, e-reader, guidebook and notebook so consider leaving the other stuff at home.

Wear bulky items in transit: Throughout the Pacific, I wore my sports sandals in transit. Wearing bulky hiking boots on a plane from Fiji to Samoa seemed like overkill. In South America, however, I was using my boots more often so decided to keep them out and wear them in transit. What a difference it made! My bag seemed almost a quarter lighter, was far more manoeuvrable and generally easier to handle. In short: it's better on your feet than on your back.

Don't forget the small stuff: It was in Tonga, three months into our trip, that I realised I was carrying 14 British pound coins in my wallet. Coins – which most countries do not exchange. I found myself in a dilemma: do I just dump £14 or do I carry it around for another nine months? Luckily, we met fellow Brit Mandy on 'Eua Island who was heading back to Britain after five years abroad. I happily gave her the coins as a parting gift. Don't forget the small stuff like emptying your wallet of change, library cards, loyalty cards, gym membership and other paraphernalia you won't use for the year. Every little helps.

Try it out for 20 minutes: Before we left home, I tried on my backpack and went for a 20-minute walk. This was an excellent way to familiarise myself with the various straps and adjustments and also good encouragement to shed more stuff. As a rule of thumb, you should be able to lift your own bag onto your back without help, lift it above your head for storage and walk with it on for 20 minutes. If you can't do this at home, you won't be able to do it in hotter climes, at altitude or on uneven terrain. You may hope to avoid walking with the backpack for any length of time but it will likely be necessary at some point – just as it was for us in Fiji and Bolivia.

If you're genuinely frightened you've left too much behind, you're probably right on the mark.

23. Buy waterproofing

Trekking across Scotland is the best way to learn about waterproofing. In Scotland, it rains. You can have a good run but eventually, in Scotland, it rains.

And after six days of glorious sunshine, on the final day of an eight-mile trek out of the Highlands, it started to rain. We didn't make it out the Highlands that day – the going was too slow and too miserable that by mid-afternoon we called it a day and set up our tents in the downpour.

Our sleeping bags were soaked through. Our camera by some miracle had survived the drenching. It was a cold and damp night's sleep that night. Before we travelled or trekked again, we bought some waterproof stuffsacs in a range of sizes for our sleeping bags, clothing and electronics, which have been invaluable. Aquapac have some great products.

It's also a good idea to have some lo-fi solutions to hand. When our hiking boots were wet through on our Machu Picchu trek, we resorted to wrapping plastic bags around our socks.

24. Double-check your problem spots

When you're packing up and moving on mid trip, always double-check the bathroom and the plug sockets. These two areas are prime for leaving things behind, namely your toiletries and travel adaptors.

If you have different trouble zones, make a mental note and always double-check them when you're moving on.

25. Leave the guitar at home

If you travel with a guitar, you'll look like a douche. At least a dozen people proved this rule on our first trip around the world. Just don't do it.

The same goes for a ukulele. In fact, let's just throw all string-based instruments in there, shall we?

CHAPTER 4: BUDGETING

26. How to save for your trip around the world

The first thing to do is calculate how much you will need using the formula given in tip 1. Once you have a target, take the below steps to quickly grow your travel fund.

Ask for a pay rise: If you are good at what you do, then be bold and ask for a pay rise. Quality employees are harder to come by than you think and most companies will do as much as possible to hang onto their best people.

Move in together: If you're travelling with someone and don't yet live together, consider doing so. It will likely have the biggest impact on your budget overall.

Give up your vices: Thankfully, my biggest vice is cheap: chocolate. Peter's, on the other hand, were slightly more fiscally demanding shall we say. There was the morning coffee habit, his penchant for Scottish whisky and his smoking of various varieties. He gave up all but the coffee and put the extra money into the travel fund. Do the same and you'll see your fund grow surprisingly quickly.

Set limits on eating out: In our year of saving, we vowed to eat out no more than twice a month including takeout. We broke the rule occasionally but in general it worked because it gave us something to look forward to. Having a quota can go a long way in strengthening your resolve.

Cancel your subscriptions: I cancelled my Spotify, Sky+ and Lovefilm subscriptions. Peter cancelled his National Geographic and Sight and Sound magazine subscriptions. Sure, it was a blip in the budget but every little helped. Ask yourself if you really need your subscriptions (especially the gym!) and if not, cancel them!

Seek free entertainment: This ties in with the point above. Instead of Spotify, use playlists on YouTube. Instead of buying books, use Project Gutenberg which offers thousands of classics for free. Instead of the gym, get a running app and get on the road. At every juncture, ask yourself: 'is this worth a day on the road?' More often than not, the answer will be no.

Rent out your spare space: If you have a spare room, rent it out. If you don't have a spare room, rent it out! In our year of saving, Peter and I lived in my one-bedroom flat. This didn't stop us putting up my living room on Airbnb as a 'shared room' with guests having the room to themselves between 9pm and 9am. We doubted we'd get any interest but ended up with a steady stream of guests and met tons of interesting people in the process. This isn't for everyone, but if you really need to squeeze out every last penny, this is a great way to do it. I also rented out my parking space, so if you have one spare, put it up on Gumtree.

Buy an annual travelcard: If you live in a city like London, you may be able to get a hefty discount on your travel fare by buying a travelcard for an extended period. For example, buying a 12-month travelcard instead of a monthly one saved me just under $400. If your company doesn't offer a season ticket loan, consider dipping into your savings for it. The money you'll save will likely outstrip any interest you'll make on the amount.

Sell your stuff: We put up a whole lot of (mainly fitness-based) items on Gumtree. There was my treadmill, Peter's rowing machine, his dumbbells and also an old 4-track from his university days. This had the added advantage of saving storage space. If you don't need it, put it up on Gumtree or Craigslist. Just give it a try.

Try to get free storage: Luckily for us, Peter's parents offered (okay, agreed) to store our stuff during our year away. Ask around to see if your friends and family have spare space to store your belongings. As we said above, every little helps.

27. Get a travel credit card

Applying for a travel credit card can be laborious but it really, really is worth it. Before we left, I applied for the Halifax Clarity Card. Alas, my application was declined because I had never before had a credit card.

There wasn't enough time for Peter to apply so we left with a credit card that was fee-free only on purchases as opposed to cash withdrawals. A 3% charge on the £20,000 ($31,000) we saved for a year of travel is £600 ($950), so that was a hefty price to pay.

Our advice is to apply at least three months before your departure. It would be prudent to start building up your air miles too. Find out more about travel and airline credit cards at Money Saving Expert: moneysavingexpert.com/credit-cards/travel-credit-cards.

28. Don't be complacent with your beginning budget

The most expensive meal of our entire trip was in our first week of travel. Yes, we had cause for celebration and, yes, the gorgeous weather and utter beauty of Vanuatu had us lulled into a honeymoon headiness, but spending $80 on a distinctly mediocre meal at Breakas Beach Resort was completely unnecessary.

We always knew our budget would tighten over the course of the trip, but we shouldn't have taken that as license to spend so freely at the start. It's important to keep costs down right from the very beginning.

29. Avoid expat supermarkets

In Vanuatu's Port Vila, we stopped off at Au Bon Marché supermarket. To our horror, we came upon $10 boxes of cereal and $7 packs of tea. We needed supplies so cherry-picked the cheapest groceries and hotfooted it out of there. A day later, we discovered a street market just metres away from the supermarket where fruit, veg and other supplies were less than half the price. Avoid western style supermarkets and opt instead for street markets and local food stands. Ask a local where they shop and follow their example.

30. Research tipping etiquette

Tipping is the number one thing we hate about travelling – not because of the cost but because of the unbearable awkwardness of the whole thing.

It's the horror of not knowing. In some cities it seems that everyone and his uncle expects a tip simply for letting you breathe in their area code (Marrakech, anyone?). In others, the locals seem incredibly embarrassed by the gesture. For example, our cab driver in Jordan refused to take a tip, as did the cleaner who found and turned in Peter's lost phone. "Please – I'm just doing my job," he insisted.

Consult your guidebook or search online for local tipping etiquette. It may not eradicate the awkwardness but will help somewhat. Finally, always hang on to small change and bills whenever you can – they always come in use.

31. Don't be shy about asking for discounts

Peter jokes that I am exceedingly British except when it comes to discounts. Then, I shrug off my British reserve with all the zeal of an Indian auntie haggling over aubergines on a street corner. I'll tell you what though: it works.

We were in a phone repair shop in LA when Peter nudged me teasingly and said, "This isn't Whitechapel Market."

I had just asked for a discount on my $70 phone repair and the guy behind the counter had apologetically refused. However, one hour later when we came to collect the phone, he winked at us and applied his employee discount. Peter was gobsmacked and I was very self satisfied. Moral of the story: always ask for discounts!

32. Take USD

Whether you like it or not, the US dollar is the currency of the world, so always keep some with you.

We try to keep a $100 reserve with us wherever possible. It often comes in use whether it's converting to local currency, covering an unexpected charge or handing out a tip at the end of a multi-day tour. Naturally, you need to make sure you don't lose it!

Our friend Marcus once told us that he used to roll up a $100 bill and hide it in the lining of his backpack whenever he went travelling. He never needed it but said he always felt better knowing it was there "just in case".

Unfortunately for him, the only time it would have come in use was when his entire backpack was stolen on a bus in Colombia.

"I bet the bastards never even found it," he told us later.

33. Be careful when changing money

Local exchange rates can vary wildly. Generally speaking, the worst rates will be at the airport, closely followed by major international banks and the business desks at large international hotel chains.

To find the best exchange rate, ask for direction at your independent hotel or hostel. It's also worth speaking to other travellers who may have some insider tips to share.

These tips can save you a sizable chunk of money. For example, in Argentina, it's far more cost effective to take US dollars into the country and exchange them on the street rather than at the bank or by withdrawing currency from ATMs. There is an official exchange rate and an "unofficial" one called the "blue rate", which is reserved for exchanging USD directly into local pesos at a much better rate.

This sort of information is often unavailable in tourist offices so it's always worth doing your own "unofficial" research.

34. Take sleeper trains

Where possible, take trains and buses that travel overnight rather than during the day. This way, you can save on a night's accommodation.

It was this logic that persuaded us to book a last-minute luxury cruise from Tahiti to LA. While a flight would have cost $800, the cruise was only $200 more expensive but included 16 nights of accommodation. Bearing in mind we were spending approximately $40 on accommodation every night, 16 nights equated to $640. Throw in Pacific Ocean views and delicious food, and we were sold!

35. Don't be daunted by pricey destinations

During the course of our trip, we went to Tahiti, Bora Bora (twice), Hawaii, the Galápagos Islands and Easter Island. Yes, they were more expensive than say Peru and Bolivia, but they didn't break the bank.

Don't be daunted as you *can* keep costs down. Visit in the shoulder seasons, root out cheap accommodation on booking.com or Airbnb (airbnb.com), fill up at breakfast so you wont need a big lunch, use public buses and ferries, hire bicycles to get around and do tours yourself.

We have specific DIY guides for the Galápagos (atlasandboots.com/galapagos-on-a-budget) and Bora Bora (atlasandboots.com/bora-bora-on-a-budget) and are available on social media to answers questions on other destinations.

CHAPTER 5: GETTING AROUND

36. Use air passes where possible

Whenever you plan a new leg of your trip, do some research on air passes for the country or countries you will be visiting. Air passes allow you to travel to several destinations within a country or region, usually more cheaply than individual flights.

We patchworked together flights in the South Pacific but in hindsight, should have paid closer attention to the Fiji Airways Air Pass as well as an Air Tahiti Pass.

It's worth noting that we recommend air passes in relation to *individual* regions as opposed to a broader RTW pass. We discuss the relative merits and drawbacks of an RTW pass in tip 3. RTW or plan as you go?

37. Don't plan more than 60% of your schedule

So many of us plan our days for 100% capacity. If all the trains run without delay and all our meetings finish on time and the gods smile down upon us, then we can get A, B, C… Z done today. We tend to carry this over to our vacation time, which might be fine for a two-week break in Sharm el-Sheikh, but will leave you exhausted on a long-term trip.

Instead of booking every stop along the way, leave your schedule as loose as possible. This way, when things go inevitably awry, you won't feel stressed out about things falling off your jam-packed schedule.

bus terminals

unto their own. From roadside
rawling concrete blocks in Colombia,
ipitated some of our most stressful
ie of the best insight into local life.
ngs to bear in mind when faced with
this challenge.

Shop around: There will often be multiple companies
hawking tickets to the same destination. Don't just settle for
the first one that's heading in your direction. Shop around.
Ask about prices, journey length, style of seat and any extra
facilities. You may end up on an overcrowded bus with
standing space only and no toilets, or you may get a luxury
bus with fully reclining seats and three meals included. It
pays to shop around.

Watch your bags: Bus terminals are prime locations for bag
snatchers, conmen and tricksters. Always be aware of your
belongings and don't get distracted during boarding and
alighting. You may need to put down your daypack when
retrieving your main backpack. If so, slide your foot into one
of the shoulder straps of your daypack, so that it can't be
grabbed.

Keep calm: Our bus ticket was for 8pm, platform five,
Medellín via Barranquilla. It was 8.30pm, we were on
platform five and the bus said 'Barranquilla'. Before
boarding, we wanted to make sure that it was the right bus
(i.e. that it would continue on to Medellín). We asked three
different officials but all we received in reply was 'Tranquilo'
(relax). After the fourth official, we were definitely not
feeling very tranquilo. The right bus turned up 15 minutes
later, was labelled 'Medellín' and everything was okay in the
end. We should have just listened and relaxed.

39. Always store headphones in your hand luggage

It was 2011 and we were in Cambodia on a four-hour bus journey from Phnom Penh to Siem Reap. We had the first two seats directly beneath the television. For four hours, it played a TV show featuring a character whose defining trait seemed to be shouting at the top of his unbelievably annoying voice. It sounded like someone coughing out their guts at 90 decibels right in front of your face.

We had unthinkingly left our headphones in our big backpacks, stowed away in the bowels of the bus. We endured that nauseating character for four hours and nearly went mad with frustration. We haven't made the same mistake since.

Always pack headphones and earplugs in your hand luggage. If you're on a long journey, throw in an eye mask too.

40. Don't get tricked by taxis

Before taking a taxi, try to gauge the journey cost either by asking your hotel receptionist or consulting your guidebook.

In a metered taxi, ask for an estimation of the journey cost. This will allow you to make an informed decision. It may also avoid a more 'scenic' route, as the driver will be conscious of staying within respectable boundaries of his initial estimate.

If the taxi is unmetered, agree on a price before you start the journey – preferably before you enter the taxi.

A trick we learnt on the road is to get an idea of the journey cost beforehand and then suggest it with a 'yes' at the end. 'Ocho dolares, si?' (Eight dollars, yes?) The driver will be inclined to agree. Incidentally, the opposite works just as consistently. We once asked 'Ocho dolares, no?' and the driver promptly shook his head and told us 10.

41. Take alternative transport

Use buses instead of cars, or cycles instead of buses, or walking instead of cycles. Use ferries instead of planes – perhaps even a kayak, like we did on Bora Bora.

Don't just go for the expensive and/or easy option. Indeed, choosing a budget mode of transport not only saves you money but also offers a host of ancillary benefits.

While travelling on a budget, we have been invited to dinner with a local family, a visit to church on Sunday, a charity horseracing event and the wedding of a first-born. Nothing like this has ever happened to us in a luxury hotel – not once.

Budget travel has also encouraged us to appreciate simple pleasures (hot showers!), made us fitter and had a halo effect on saving money; when staff and locals see that you're on a budget, they often do more to help you save costs.

42. Try hitchhiking

Hitchhiking is an individual choice and most guidebooks warn against it as a rule. It has never been our first choice of travel but we *have* done it in a pinch including in remote parts of Finland, Samoa and Tahiti where public transport was not available. Here are our best tips for newbies.

Check local laws: Hitchhiking is illegal in some areas and along certain road types, so make sure you check the rules beforehand. Ask a local if hitchhiking is common and safe. If you are carrying any substances that may cause problems with the police (tut tut), be aware that hitchhiking may attract the attention of local law enforcement.

Hitchhike with a partner: A lone hitchhiker looks like a drifter while two hitchhikers look like travelling friends, so travel with a partner if you can. Some experts swear that two females fare the best, but several hitchhikers have told us that a mixed-gender couple works better. A driver picking up two females may worry that he'll be accused of something unsavoury whereas a male-female couple seems like a safe bet with fewer complications.

Learn the right gesture: Make sure you know the local gesture for stopping a car as the thumb-up sign isn't always appropriate. In parts of the South Pacific for example you would be expected to hold out your hand, palm down, and move it up and down as if instructing the car to slow down.

Find a good location: Instead of trying to hitch from inside a city where most people will be travelling within the city limits, try your hand at the last traffic light in town or a slip road. This will increase your chances of finding a driver travelling a long distance. Ensure that drivers have plenty of time to see you and that there is a safe place for them to pull over. Use Hitchwiki (hitchwiki.org) to find out about specific locations. If your driver is taking you only part of the way, ask to be dropped off at a similarly good spot instead of the city centre.

Think twice about making a sign: On one hand, a sign is helpful as it clearly indicates where you are headed and minimises the number of false starts. However, it may also work against you: some drivers who may have taken you part of the way may not stop if they're not going all the way to your destination. Consider using general directions instead ('East' or 'West').

Wear clean clothes in bright colours: Wearing a bright colour will not only make you more visible but also more approachable. White is a good choice.

Ditch the shades: Don't wear shades or a hat; let drivers see your face. Make eye contact and offer a warm smile. This will make you seem more trustworthy and approachable.

One hitchhiker friend has a theory that keeping your forearms bare makes you seem less threatening (i.e. nothing hidden in your sleeves).

Be confident: Don't limply stick out your hand with a sheepish shrug. Stand near the road, hold your hand out high, be confident and smile. Drivers only have a few seconds to make their decision and if you're half hearted, they will be too.

Wave your thanks even if they don't stop: Smile, nod or wave thanks to drivers that make eye contact, especially if they indicate that they can't take you. It will go some way in dispelling the general fear around hitchhiking.

Be safe:

- Don't be afraid to decline a ride if the driver seems intoxicated, erratic or just plain creepy. Ask them where they're going and tell them you're going another way or say "thank you, but I'm hoping to go further."
- If you do accept a ride, note the vehicle's registration number and ideally the make, model, and color too. If possible, text the information to a friend.
- Sit in the front passenger seat if possible as the rear ones may have a child lock.
- Keep your essentials within easy reach in case you need to make a quick exit. If your big backpack is locked in the boot, be prepared to lose it.
- Keep your phone charged. Buy a solar charger to top it up on the go.
- Carry a personal safety alarm. You probably won't need it but it's best to be prepared.
- If you have accepted a ride but really want to get out of the vehicle, pretend that you need to be sick. Tell the driver not to wait, then stride off to the side of the road.

Learn some of the language: If you don't speak the local language, pick up a phrase or two beforehand. Lone drivers in particular may pick up hitchhikers for the company. A deathly awkward silence won't put either of you at ease.

Keep some sweets with you: Whether it's a pack of sweets or a bar of chocolate, having something to offer the driver is a useful way to break the ice especially if you don't speak their language.

Consider crossing borders yourself: Land borders are a good place to get a ride but bear in mind that drivers may be wary of carrying hitchhikers across borders. You may find it easier to cross the border yourself and find a ride on the other side. Note that some borders have a strip of no-man's land in between which may not be possible to cross on foot.

Always carry a good map: Even if you have Google Maps, great coverage and a fully charged phone, carry a paper map and preferably a compass too.

Have a backup plan: You may have to walk all day or pay for an overnight stay. Have a plan B wherever possible. If it means doing the same thing all over again the next day, try not to get disheartened. The key is to look happy, clean, friendly and approachable. Ask yourself 'would I pick myself up?' and amend your behaviour or appearance accordingly.

43. How to cope with babies on planes

Let's be honest: no one wants to be seated next to a crying baby on a long-haul flight.

There are tactics we can use to alleviate the issue (earplugs, headphones, whisky) but one trick works better than any of that: ask the parent if you can help in any way.

This acts as a psychological hack in that you find yourself empathising with the parent and rooting for them. Taking a child on a flight is highly stressful – especially for a parent travelling alone. Offering to help puts you on their team and switches your mindset.

If you prefer not to bother the parent, then put yourself in their shoes from a distance. Try to understand what the experience is like for them. Your irritation will hopefully(!) turn to empathy.

44. Claim compensation on delayed flights

If you've booked a flight that was cancelled or delayed by more than three hours, you may be entitled to compensation depending on the circumstances.

For a chance at success, you must be able to answer yes to the following four questions.

1. Was it an EU flight? Compensation only applies for EU flights. This is defined as a flight that departs from an EU airport (regardless of airline) or an EU airline that lands at an EU airport. This means a London to New York flight qualifies regardless of airline, but a New York to London flight won't qualify if you're flying a non-EU airline (e.g. Jet Airways).

2. Was it the airline's fault? Compensation is only payable if the delay or cancellation was caused by the airline. So, for example, bad weather, industrial action, political problems, safety issues, technical issues caused by the plane manufacturer or air traffic management decisions absolve the airline of any liability. If, however, the delay was caused by a late crew or pilot, a cancellation due to under-booking, technical problems caused by the airline or failed safety checks, then they will be liable. Find a full list of circumstances here: ec.europa.eu/transport/themes/passengers/air/doc/neb-extraordinary-circumstances-list.pdf.

3. Was the delay over three hours? Compensation is payable only on delayed arrivals of three hours or more. This means that if you left three hours late but made up five minutes in the air, landing 2hr 55m late, you will not be entitled to compensation; it's arrival time that matters. The amount of compensation depends on the distance flown and length of the delay.

- Up to 1,500km (3 hours): £210 per person
- 1,500km-3,500 km (3 hours): £335 per person
- 3,500km+ (3-4 hours): £250 per person
- 3,500km+ (4+ hours): £505 per person

Check flight distance: webflyer.com
Check if flight was delayed: flightstats.com (registration required)

4. Was the delay/cancellation after 2007? Flights after February 2005 qualify for compensation but airlines might get sneaky with pre-2007 claims as they can't be taken to court over them due to the statute of limitations.

If you can indeed answer yes to all the questions, then download and complete the flight delays (moneysavingexpert.com/redir/46eb7062) or cancellations (moneysavingexpert.com/redir/b3921b76) templates from Money Saving Expert and send it to the airline's complaints department.

Make sure you include the passenger name(s), your address, contact details, flight details (booking ref, flight no., departure airport and destination airport), flight length and your flight receipt – plus any supporting documents if you have them (boarding passes or tickets). If the airline tries to wriggle out of it, complain to the Civil Aviation Authority (caa.co.uk/passengers/resolving-travel-problems) or your corresponding national authority.

CHAPTER 6: ACCOMMODATION

45. Stay in the centre

When staying in cities or towns, opt for accommodation in or close to the centre. We were relatively lax about this rule until we booked a hostel 15 minutes out of Uyuni in Bolivia. In the day, the walk was oppressively hot; in the evening, dark, dingy and deserted. Naturally, there are exceptions to the rule but staying in the centre is the safer bet.

Here's a trusty method for booking accommodation: go to booking.com and enter your location and requested dates. Use the filters as needed and then click onto one of the listed hotels. Click 'Show map', then narrow your focus to the area(s) with a high density of accommodation options. Book one of the options with a rating of 7 or higher.

It's worth noting that ratings on booking.com are more trustworthy than TripAdvisor as it only allows reviews from people who have booked a stay through the site.

46. Use Airbnb

We've used Airbnb (airbnb.com) extensively over the years – as hosts and guests – and have developed a fairly keen sense of what constitutes good guest etiquette. Here are the essentials.

Read the entire listing – and use the calendar! Hosts dislike it when users message asking 'is your place available?' or 'is there public transport?' or 'how far is the station?' or

...ing that can be answered by a passing glance at the ...ing description. Hosts have spent time and effort putting together descriptions and the calendar is readily available so these types of questions can be time wasting and frustrating. If you need information that isn't in the description, absolutely message the host but please read the listing first.

Don't worry about an introductory message: If you have a complete profile and a good review or two, there is no need to send an introductory message before you book unless the host explicitly requests one in the listing description. If you really feel awkward about staying at someone's place without exchanging pleasantries first, then that's fine but don't feel you have to do it as par for the course. Instead, place a booking request and add an introductory note to that. This will suffice for most hosts.

Don't ask to pay in cash: Yes, we know the Airbnb fee is a pain. It's pretty hefty and we'd all be richer if we did a cash-in-hand kind of deal, but please don't ask for this. The fee is there to protect guests and hosts in terms of both monetary insurance and personal safety.

Book quickly after your enquiry: If your host has promised to reserve your dates for a short while, or has offered you a special rate, don't leave them hanging for hours. Complete your booking as soon as possible. It's obvious when guests have pinged off tons of emails to lots of hosts and are waiting for the best deal. Generally, hosts understand and appreciate that you're after value for money but if they're holding onto dates for you, it's rude to leave them hanging.

Let your host know if you're running late: Try to give your host an accurate idea of when you will be arriving. They may have plans which they have to fit around you or, if they're not staying in the same place, they will need to travel to where they'll be staying for the night. As such, if you said you'd arrive at 8pm and actually it's looking like 10pm, make sure you let your host know. Apologise for the delay and let them know you appreciate their flexibility.

Bear in mind that it's not a hotel: With Airbnb accommodation, you must remember that you are in someone's home. This means that a) not everything will be as immaculate as in a hotel because people actually live there and b) there won't be a maid cleaning up after guests. Hosts certainly won't expect you to clean the place when you leave but a decent level of tidiness is appreciated – especially if you weren't charged a cleaning fee.

Ask about a bathroom schedule: If you're sharing a home rather than booking an entire home, it may be that you end up sharing a bathroom. In this case, it is considerate to ask if the host needs it at certain times. Chances are, they will be working while you're on holiday so if they need the bathroom for half an hour in the morning before work, they'll really appreciate it if you let them have it.

Tell the host if there's something wrong: If you're unhappy with something, tell the host as early as possible. Most hosts will bend over backwards to help their guests so please be honest if something is wrong. What you shouldn't do is stay silent on an issue and only mention it in your post-stay review. By all means, mention it in your review if your complaint isn't dealt with fairly but you shouldn't pretend everything is okay only to complain later.

Be considerate about additional guests: If you book a room for one person, don't assume that someone else can stay with you – especially if you're sharing the home with your host. If it's a long-term stay and you've gotten to know them, maybe it's okay to ask. If it's a short stay, however, it's cheeky especially as some hosts charge for a second guest.

Leave a review (quickly): This is an obvious one but when a host has opened up their home to you, they really appreciate it when you leave a review soon after your stay. Read tip 48. Add honest reviews.

You don't need to tip your host: Tipping is a way of showing appreciation for good service, but Airbnb/housesitting hosts don't see what they're doing as a service as such – rather, they're sharing their home with you as an equal. You and they co-exist in the same space; they do not "serve" you in the same way that hotel staff might do. As such, there is no need to tip them. If you want to show your appreciation, a small gift such as a box of chocolates or even just a note would be more appropriate.

47. Report problems immediately

We knew Copacabana in Bolivia wasn't the Copacabana of the song but would have been happy with a simulacrum of charm. Unfortunately, the lakeside town represents much that is wrong with tourism. Pushy restaurateurs force their staff to solicit diners on the street, ticket agents are stacked like sardines and grumpy women flog fake sunglasses on street corners.

To make matters worse, we had chosen a hostel poorly. On first glance, the room was basic but just about serviceable. However, when we returned in the evening, we discovered that there wasn't any water in the taps or toilet. We were used to cold showers but no water at all was pushing it. Reception was closed up with no one around and we were exhausted, so we turned in and hoped the problem would be solved in the morning.

It wasn't.

We reported it to the owner's wife, then waited an hour for the problem to be fixed. We took lightning quick showers to catch our boat and complained to the owner on checkout. He accused us of lying and then tested the water to prove that it did indeed work – all while his wife stood by dutifully mute.

We had neither the time nor the language skills to argue effectively so paid the bill in full and left.

The lesson we learnt: report a problem as soon as it arises, even if it means hunting down the hotelier after reception has closed. If worse comes to worst, make a video recording of the problem so you have evidence and make a complaint via the booking site if necessary.

48. Add honest reviews

It's relatively easy to give a scuzzy hostel or overpriced hotel a bad review. More often than not, the owner is a faceless entity profiting off their subpar facilities.

With sites like Airbnb, however, you meet your hosts face to face and often share their home with them. You may meet their partners and families and eat at their table, so it's natural to feel bad about leaving them negative feedback. But here's the thing: if we're all polite about everybody, the reviews lose their meaning.

It's essential to leave honest and accurate reviews for all services you use, whether it's a faceless hotel chain or a very personal experience. It might make you uncomfortable, but trust in the fact that you're contributing to the overall usefulness and quality of the site.

As for *reading* reviews, pay attention to star ratings. Often, the reviews are personalised but the ratings are anonymised and swallowed into the overall average, so guests are likely to be more honest in their ratings.

CHAPTER 7: OUTDOOR

49. How to choose the right hiking boots

Know your requirements: Will you be going on short day hikes, multi-day treks or high-altitude expeditions? How cold and wet is it likely to get? Will it be soft underfoot, hard rock or loose scree? Research the terrain before you buy.

Ankle support: On smooth terrain, a good pair of trainers will do just fine. On rough or slippery terrain, however, hiking boots are the far better choice. When darting over loose rocks or grappling for footing amid big boulders, it's deceptively easy to fall and snap an ankle. You have a choice between low-, mid- and high-cut ankle support. The higher the support the more roll-resistance you'll have for your ankles.

Waterproof: There are few things more miserable than soggy socks on a multi-day trek. On such a trek across the South Downs one winter, I (Peter) found my aging lightweight fabric boots letting in water despite full-length ankle gaiters, so I made the painful decision to finally retire them. Thankfully, my new leather pair proved 100% waterproof on a springtime trek across Dartmoor. Check the spec of your boots' membrane to make sure they're waterproof (or prepare yourself for the old English tradition we call soggy socks). There's a trade-off between leather and fabric; between waterproofness and breathability.

Flexibility: While durability is essential, flexibility is important too. Unless you're attaching crampons, you probably want something pretty flexible. Kia was initially tempted to buy a pair as heavy duty as mine. She tried on the Anatom V3, insisting they were comfortable. Luckily, one of the in-store experts pointed out that the boots were too stiff for her petite feet. He prodded the tip, showing her that she could barely bend her toes. He suggested a more lightweight pair, which were perfect (the Anatom V2). When trying on your boots, spend a few minutes walking around in them and make sure you can bend your toes. Otherwise, a long hike will quickly become unbearable.

Weight: My hiking boots are one of the heaviest items in my bag so be aware of this when choosing yours. Don't automatically opt for the most durable pair. If you'll only be going on leisure hikes, you don't need an extra two kilos on your feet. For men, depending on your size, up to about 1,800 grams is acceptable. For women, I suggest between 1,200 and 1,500. Don't pay too much attention to the figures; the important thing is to get into a shop and try on different pairs to see what suits you.

Space: It's important that your boots fit you well but make sure they're not overly snug. Put on a thick pair of socks when trying on your boots to make sure they can be accommodated. Thick socks are essential on long hikes, even in hot weather. If you wear them with thin socks or, even worse, trainer socks, they will likely chafe, cause blisters and quickly become uncomfortable.

50. How to find a good camping spot

Choose flat ground: First and most obvious in getting a comfortable night's sleep is to make sure you pitch your tent on flat ground. Unfortunately, nature isn't always accommodating so if you must pitch on a slope, pitch your tent in a way so you can sleep with your head at the top of the slope. Ground that has a slight incline will help to avoid puddles in case it rains. And it often does.

Check the surface: Rocks, roots, branches, rubble and stones are all ingredients for a torn groundsheet and an uncomfortable night's sleep. It's fine to clear your area but, in general, if it doesn't look good then it probably isn't good. Try to find a clear surface to begin with and save yourself the hassle.

Find shelter or windbreaks: If you can find a natural windbreak for your pitch then it will make life a lot easier – especially when you're putting up your tent. Hedges, fences, large boulders, rock outcroppings or small crops of trees will all offer protection from wind. Just make sure you're not camping under a potential rockslide! Trees can offer protection from the wind, but do note that a lone tall tree can be a beacon for a lightning strike. Dense stands of trees, all a similar height, in a relatively low area away from water offer the best protection from lightning. If you're winter camping, avoid setting up under trees with snow on their branches.

Water supply: You should always practise low-impact camping and avoid contaminating any water supplies. If you're wild camping, always pitch at least 60 metres (200ft) away from your water supply. That said, easy access to water is essential so don't pitch too far away either. On a campsite, don't be tempted to pitch too close to the water supply as this is a high-traffic area.

Avoid compacted ground: Don't pick a spot just because others have camped there. When people camp on the same site over and over, the ground underneath gets compacted. This can be bad news if it rains heavily. You can find your campsite suddenly swamped when the compacted area fills up with water. Don't pitch your tent in one of these overused indentations, or any indentation for that matter!

Toilets: The worst thing about camping is getting up in the middle of the night and having to walk to the toilet block, but this is usually the busiest area so if you don't want people traipsing past your tent all night, pitch a fair distance away. Just be prepared for a long, cold walk in the night. If you're wild camping, make sure your waste has minimum impact on the environment. Always bury everything.

Consider the sun: Personally, I (Peter) like to thaw out in my tent as the morning breaks so if you're like me and want the morning sun to warm you up, make sure your campsite faces south (in the northern hemisphere). If you're planning to spend time in your tent during the day then make sure you'll have some shade. A tent can easily turn into a sauna during the hottest part of the day.

Be aware of hazards: Is your campsite safe from hazards such as rock falls, flash floods, high tide or avalanches? As mentioned, natural windbreaks can be really useful but also come with their own set of hazards. You need to be aware of the local environment and avoid camping somewhere you can get hurt, especially in the wild where there may not be help for miles around.

Good campsites are found, not made: This goes hand in hand with much of the above. Remember the reason we go camping is to enjoy nature in all its beauty and glory. Always be mindful of your local environment and try to leave it exactly as you found it. This is especially important if you're wild camping. Try to pitch late, leave early and, of course, leave no trace (lnt.org/learn/seven-principles-overview).

51. How to use a map and compass

Features of a compass

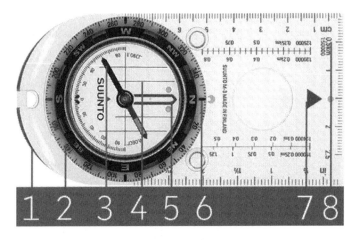

1. **Base plate:** the transparent plastic base.
2. **Bezel/compass housing:** the grooved ring encompassing the compass needle. It usually has a mark every two degrees covering 360 degrees as well as the four main compass points (N-S-E-W).
3. **Compass needle:** the red end on any compass will always point north. It floats on liquid so it can rotate freely.
4. **Orientating/compass lines:** the lines on the bottom of the baseplate.
5. **Orientating arrow:** fixed and aligned to north inside the bezel/compass housing.
6. **Index line:** basically an extension of the direction of travel arrow (7) and is fixed within the outer edge.
7. **Direction of travel arrow:** the big arrow at the end of the base plate.
8. **Map and compass scales:** 1:25,000, 1:50,000 and metric measurer (known as Romer scales).

Finding north: There is a difference between magnetic north on the compass and grid north on your map. This varies in different areas of the world, so depending where you are and the distance you are covering, be prepared for it to affect your navigation.

The needle on your compass always points to magnetic north. Information about this 'magnetic declination' is usually printed on hiking maps (e.g. Ordnance Survey) which will tell you how much to account for. In most of the UK, the difference is roughly two degrees, so you should adjust your compass by turning the bezel anticlockwise two degrees. You may wish to mark this point with tape or a marker.

In some parts of the world, the difference can be as much as 20 degrees. Make sure you know the magnetic declination in the area and if your map doesn't have it, get a better one!

Using a compass

There are four main uses of a compass: determine your heading, set the map, take a bearing, follow a bearing.

Determine your heading: Hold the compass out in front of your chest with the direction of travel arrow pointing in the direction you're heading. Rotate the bezel so that N aligns with the red end of the compass needle. The number (in degrees) on the rim of the bezel at the index line is your heading.

Set the map: You need to set the map with your compass, aligning it so that it corresponds to the surrounding landscape.

- Lay the map out flat in front of you
- Put the compass anywhere on top of the map
- Turn the map and compass until the needle on the

compass aligns with the north-south gridlines on the map – the red end of the needle must be pointing to the top of the map

Take a bearing

- Find a feature on the map that you want to head towards
- Identify this feature on the ground
- Lay the compass on the map so that orientating lines on the compass point align with your route towards the feature on the map
- Without moving the map or compass, rotate the bezel so that the orientating arrow points towards north on the map – the number (in degrees) on the rim of the bezel at the index line is the bearing you need to follow
- Remove the compass from the map and hold it with the direction of travel arrow pointing straight away from you
- Rotate your body, including the compass, until the red end of the needle lies within the orientating arrow
- The direction of travel arrow should now point towards the feature or destination – that's the bearing you're going to follow

Follow a bearing: Follow the direction indicated by the direction of travel arrow until you reach your feature or destination. Continue to check your bearing along the way by constantly checking your direction of travel needle. If possible, identify features on the ground which are along your direction of travel and on your map.

52. How to build a campfire

Many a man claims to be an expert fire starter – in the same way many a man claims he does not need to ask for directions

Alpha male or not, nothing should get between a camper and a glorious night spent around a campfire beneath the stars. Here's where to start.

Position your campfire: First things first, position your campfire at least three metres (10ft) away from anything flammable like your tent or overhanging trees. Ideally, the area will be sheltered from the wind but always leave enough distance to protect yourself and the environment. Look for flat ground on which to build your campfire to prevent flaming embers from rolling down the hillside.

Create your fire bed: If your campsite has designated firepits, always use them. If you're wild camping, use a pre-existing fire bed whenever possible. Naturally, there will be occasions on which you have to make your own. Your fire bed should be on exposed earth and not grass (especially dead grass). If you can't find an area like this, you can dig away grass and plant material or pile up some dirt into a small platform (always check local guidelines first). Give your fire plenty of space by creating a large bed for it as dry grass, branches and plant material can all be a hazard.

Create a ring of rocks: It's good practice to use a ring of rocks to help contain the fire. Use dry rocks about the size of a clenched fist and space them apart so some air can still circulate at the bottom of the fire. Don't build your fire against large boulders or objects as it will leave unsightly marks. Also, avoid using damp or wet rocks as they can spit moisture and even fracture as they heat up.

Gather your wood: It goes without saying that you want dry wood. Avoid anything that is green, too wet or that bends without snapping – it almost certainly won't burn well. Try to use only fallen wood – this is better for the environment and burns more effectively too. Always collect more tinder and kindling than you think you'll need; it burns quickly and if you run out early on, your fire will never get going.

Tinder: Every good campfire starts with good tinder. Tinder should catch fire easily and burn fast. Material such as dry leaves, grass, bark and wood shavings all work well. If you're a smart camper, you'll bring your own tinder such as dryer lint, char cloth or firelighters.

Kindling: You can't move directly from tinder to your main fuel such as logs as this will smother your fire. Like tinder, kindling needs to be as dry as possible or it won't burn as easily. Try to find small twigs and branches about the length and width of a pencil. If you're struggling to find dry kindling, you can use your penknife (of course you have a penknife) to whittle down larger damp twigs and branches to get to the drier timber underneath.

Fuel: Unlike tinder and kindling, you can get away with your fuel wood being a little damp. A well-built fire will dry it out (but it's still not ideal). You'll want a range of different sized branches and logs for your main fuel – not just woodsman-sized logs. Gather a range of branches and logs that are roughly as wide as your wrist or your forearm.

Lay your fire: There are several ways to lay your fire depending on what your needs are. Nearly all start with either a tepee or lean-to fire lay.

- **Tepee:** Place a bundle of tinder in the centre of your fire bed and then build a tepee around it using your kindling. Leave a small gap for lighting and to let air in.

Gradually build this up with kindling and then add some smaller fuel wood. With both the kindling and the fuel wood, try to keep the thicker ends at the bottom.

- **Lean-to:** Stick a long piece of kindling into the ground at about a 30-degree angle – this will be your support stick. It can also be leaned against a bigger log instead. Bundle tinder and some smaller kindling under the support stick before laying kindling against it around the outside. Add another layer.

Light your fire: When lighting your campfire you want to alight the tinder right in the centre as quickly as possible. Matches can get wet and easily blow out outdoors. Cigarette lighters are not ideal for getting right inside the tinder bundle but are better than matches. We use Zippo's Flex Neck Utility Lighter which has a wind-resistant flame, ideal for lighting campfires in all conditions.

Build up and add to your fire: Once your fire is going, it's time to build it up. You have a number of choices depending on your needs. Whichever method you choose, build up your campfire slowly and steadily, working through your fuel from the thinner branches up to the larger logs.

Extinguish your fire: This is the saddest part of an evening around a campfire but it's also crucial. Give yourself plenty of time and start to extinguish your fire at least 20 minutes before you want to be tucked in your sleeping bag. Hopefully, you have allowed your campfire to die down so it's no longer roaring. Lightly sprinkle water onto the fire bed and stir the embers and ashes with a stick. Heat test the fire by holding the back of your hand close to it. If it's too hot to keep your hand there, the fire is still too hot to leave. Continue to sprinkle water and stir until safe to leave.

Leave no trace: Finally, practise the Leave No Trace Seven Principles (lnt.org/learn/seven-principles-overview) and minimise the impact of your campfires by patching up any disturbed ground. Most importantly, always know and follow the fire regulations of the area you're visiting.

53. You don't need to shower every day

It was on day two of my first camping experience that I (Kia) lost my temper in grand old style. The wild dogs, the crawling commode and the freezing cold showers negated the beauty of our right-on-the-beach camping spot on Taveuni, Fiji's beautiful garden island. We were only a month into our trip and I was still wedded to the concept of a daily shower even though it was a painful experience in most budget places.

It was several months later on our Machu Picchu trek that I finally gave up and accepted that sometimes a daily shower just isn't necessary. Instead of washing in exposed showers with freezing water and near-zero pressure, I opted for wet wipes and talcum powder (an effective alternative to dry shampoo). This made the camping experience far more tolerable for me. (Naturally, Peter was having a whale of a time.)

You don't need to shower every day – especially when camping. The sooner you accept this, the less pain you'll endure.

CHAPTER 8: CULTURE SHOCK

54. Always ask nicely

The worst thing about that night was that we had switched hostels. Our first had been perfectly fine – clean, warm showers, helpful staff – but it was a 20-minute walk into central Baños in Ecuador and we wanted to be closer. Santa Cruz hostel seemed like a nice, well-equipped place. We were given a room directly next to the communal firepit, but it did say it shut down "strictly and with no exceptions" at 11pm.

Cue the most obnoxiously loud American man we've ever encountered, three high-pitched Valley girls whose entire vocabulary seemed restricted to the word "like" and a firepit that certainly did not shut down at 11pm – and you have a recipe for the worst night's sleep of your life.

In the early hours, Peter's patience broke and he stormed out to tell them to quieten down. As a former teacher, he immediately realised his mistake. Instead of quieting, like children they started mimicking him with witty comments such as "Hey guys, can you be quiet? I'm banging my girlfriend." Why they thought it was insulting to imply he was a stud we'll never know…

The moral is of course to ask nicely first.

55. Be assertive with dietary requirements

I (Kia) haven't eaten meat since I was 13 so you can imagine my predicament when visiting some of the most carnivorous countries in the world (Argentina, Chile, Brazil).

Maybe it's my *I-don't-want-to-make-a-fuss* Britishness or the *you-don't-get-Muslim-vegetarians!!!* reaction I received from relatives throughout my youth, but I've always been somewhat embarrassed by the fact that I don't eat meat.

In South America, this manifested in quietly searching out veggie dishes in restaurants instead of asking for recommendations or requesting custom dishes. As a result, I'd often end up with a bland, overly-cheesy pizza instead of the many delicious dishes on offer, many of which could have been adapted for vegetarians.

Be assertive with your dietary requirements. If the restaurant can't fulfil your request, chances are they will feel more sheepish about it than you. Don't be afraid to go off menu. The worst that can happen is that you're told no in which case you apologise with a smile and just go somewhere else. No harm done at all.☐

56. Double-check unlabelled prices

In shops and restaurants, if the price of a product is not written down, check and double-check it. This is especially important in restaurants which don't have written menus. After all, you can walk away from a shop if the vendor hikes the price; you can't do the same after you've already eaten.

If you place your order with a different person to the one who quoted the price, check it again. We learnt this lesson the painful way in Areguá, Paraguay.

At La Cocina de Gulliver, we were greeted by a portly woman with a broom in hand. She told us they didn't have menus, so we asked what was on offer and listened carefully to the list.

We asked for the price of paella and she said, "Noventa mil."

"Noventa mil?" we checked.

"Si. Noventa mil."

At $15, it was pricier than our budget would allow but we were sticky and exhausted so decided to indulge. She led us to a table at the back at which point a waitress came and took our order. We opted for the seafood paella (which incidentally came with chunks of chicken which Kia doesn't eat!).

After an underwhelming meal, we asked for the bill which came to an unexpected total of $40 – nearly three times what was quoted. When we queried this, the waitress shrugged and said the first woman would not have told us noventa mil because the dish cost a lot more. Naturally, the first woman had conveniently disappeared. It was a complete stitch up, which we may or may not have avoided had we rechecked the price with the waitress.

57. Travel responsibly

Responsible travel can be split into three categories: environmental, social and economic.

Environmental

Minimise your carbon footprint: Travel by train, bus or boat instead of driving. Even better, walk or cycle where possible. If you must drive, try to carpool with fellow travellers. Be mindful of using natural resources. Use water sparingly and recycle where possible.

Respect wildlife: Don't encourage unethical animal tourism. Never ride elephants or pet sedated predators. A stoned tiger on your lap might make for a good Facebook photo but it encourages deeply unethical practices.

Obey local rules: Whether it's going off trail, feeding wild animals or picking shells from the beach, never break local rules. These are designed to limit the impact of tourism and it is intrinsic that they be followed.

Leave no trace: This refers to a set of outdoor ethics promoting conservation in the outdoors. It lists seven principles that should be adhered to at all times.

- Plan ahead and prepare
- Travel and camp on durable surfaces
- Dispose of waste properly
- Leave what you find
- Minimise campfire impacts
- Respect wildlife
- Be considerate of other visitors

Social

Respect local etiquette: If you're turned away at Angkor Wat for not covering your shoulders, don't roll your eyes at the parochialism of it all; come back with a t-shirt on. Research local etiquette. Some customs will grate on your sensibilities but you must show respect.

Don't give money to working children: Saying no to begging or working children may tug on your heartstrings but it's the more ethical choice overall. Giving money only encourages their carers to keep them on the street, so invest in sustainable projects instead.

Economic

Stay at local lodgings: It's always easier to stay with the Aussie expats who speak English, but opt for local lodgings where possible. This invests in the local community and offers a more authentic experience.

Opt for responsible companies: Where possible, use companies and organisations that invest in the local community. For example, Friends International in Cambodia runs a set of restaurants that train vulnerable youth in hospitality. Daughters of Cambodia cafe rescues women from sex trafficking. Root out local projects and services that perform a greater good.

58. Spend time with locals

"When you travel, remember that a foreign country is not designed to make you comfortable. It is designed to make its own people comfortable," said American author Clifton Fadiman.

The people of a country chiefly define its character and soul. If you really want to get to know a country then you have to get to know its people – often easier said than done.

Try to book local accommodation, eat where locals eat and shop where they shop. Go to festivals, markets and religious ceremonies and learn some of the local language too.

In Samoa, we stayed with a local family in one of their beach fales where we interacted with them every day. We had meals with our hosts, went to church with them, met their family and even drove their children to school one day.

This level of interaction isn't always possible, but sites like HelpX (helpx.net), Homestay (homestay.com) and Airbnb (airbnb.com) will certainly provide better opportunity than Expedia and its ilk.

59. Accept invitations outside your comfort zone

Both Peter and I have tricky relationships with religion. He was brought up as a Methodist Christian but became an atheist in his early twenties. I was born a Muslim which was problematic for a girl who always wanted to see the world.

With this in mind, when a local Samoan family invited us to the Sunday service at their Catholic church, we both took pause. It was a great opportunity to experience some Samoan culture, but we weren't sure if our attendance was appropriate.

As if on cue, Lena, our host, said: "Don't worry if you are not Catholic. We welcome all people in our church." Then, with a smile, she added: "There's a free lunch after."

With our reserve put to rest, we accepted the invitation.

As the service started, I felt Peter shift beside me. For me, this was a charming cultural experience; for him, it was a reminder of childhood and the ensuing confusion he felt about his faith. The language may have been different but the sentiment was the same. Later, when he recognised the cadence of the Lord's Prayer, I saw him mouth along to it in English and join in the punctuating 'Amen'. I guess some things are more enduring than we think.

I watched as members of the congregation kneeled, crossed themselves, prayed and sang. At one point, our normally vivacious host had tears rolling down her face. It reminded me that religion, for all its ills, also brings comfort and solace to much of the world's population.

It was a bittersweet moment we would have missed had we declined the invitation.

60. Be prepared to haggle

Further to tip 31. Don't be shy about asking for discounts, be prepared to haggle in local stores and markets. Most items are marked up for tourists and many vendors will *expect* you to haggle.

Before you ask for a price, mentally set a preferred price as well as a ceiling price for what you would be willing to pay. This avoids the anchoring effect.

Author and psychologist Daniel Kahneman describes the anchoring effect in Thinking Fast and Slow as the human tendency to rely too heavily on the first piece of information offered (the "anchor") when making decisions. If the vendor names an astronomical price, that price becomes the anchor and chances are you will gravitate up towards it. If you pre-set a ceiling, you will know beforehand how much is too much and will avoid reaching up towards the anchor.

Pre-setting a preferred price also helps as you won't feel compelled to keep haggling the vendor below what you feel is fair. After all, they're just trying to make a living. If you can't reach agreement, smile, say thank you and head towards the door. If you're lucky, they'll call you back in.

61. Be prepared to bribe

Sadly, bribing is a mainstay of tourism in a number of countries. Often, the demand for a bribe will be presented as an administration fee, fine, penalty or other euphemism.

In official settings (border crossing, immigration office, police stop), it's easier to pay the bribe than to argue. In others (tourist hotspots in Egypt), demands for 'baksheesh' can be ignored – simply walk away.

Keep change and small dollar amounts on you at all times, separate to your main stash of cash. Before you hand it over, however, try playing the dumb tourist first. If you can't understand what they want, they may just leave you alone.

62. Check your privilege

When times are stressful, try to remember that you are one of the most privileged people in the world. The mere fact that you can travel, that you can speak English, that you have at least a basic education already puts you leaps and bounds ahead of the majority of the world's population.

I (Kia) have been reminded of this time and again on our travels. The reason I (and most likely you) have achieved anything is not mainly due to intelligence but circumstance; a privilege supplied by the country of our birth or the wealth of our families.

I've met people on the road who could very well be running multinational companies had they been born elsewhere. There was Werry on Vanuatu's Tanna Island, Josie the receptionist at Poseidon Dive Centre in Colombia's Taganga and Amirico, a guide on the Salkantay trek in Peru. All these people had an intelligence and ability that shone as bright as any graduate or executive I've met at home, but they will never have the opportunities that I've had.

Privilege is so often invisible to those who have it. It provides us security and strokes our egos and lays claim to achievements that aren't fully ours. Travel is the most effective way I've found to pull privilege into the light, to give it shape and tangible form, to force us to accept one simple truth: that you and I are far more lucky than we are smart.

CHAPTER 9: WELLBEING

63. Learn to talk to strangers

I (Peter) wasn't always confident when talking to strangers but solo trips through India, Africa and Europe changed that. While I was comfortable spending time on my own, I didn't want to do it 24/7 and so had to learn to talk to people I didn't know. Here are the tips I use to break the ice and endear myself to the unacquainted.

Use names – theirs and yours: Use the other person's name several times in conversation to establish a bond. It's a little 'telesales-y', but it works. It shows that you are listening and are focused on them. A less common trick I use is to mention my own name in conversation. For example, if we're talking about travelling, I might say: "My girlfriend doesn't like camping unfortunately. She'll insist that she'll be fine but within five minutes it's 'Peter, I'm cold!'"

This reminds the other person of your name, something easily forgotten in a rushed introduction. It saves them the embarrassment of asking your name again or, worse, the awkwardness of talking to you for 20 minutes without the faintest clue what you're called.

Choose groups over individuals: It's always easier to initiate a conversation with another lone person, but where possible opt for groups instead. It's far easier to maintain an interesting conversation with three or more people than it is with two. In a group, no one is left wondering if they'll be stuck talking to one person all night; everyone has the option to leave the group and mingle with others with no fear of being rude. You might be reluctant to approach a pair but just because two people are at a party or on the road together, it doesn't mean they don't want to meet other people.

Don't be *that* guy: He knows something about everything and never nothing about something. He's done your job and he probably did it better than you. He's been where you went on holiday last week… twice. And while he was there he climbed the same mountain you did, but he done it in half the time… and paraglided off the summit at midnight.

We've all met one of these guys and – as the saying goes – if you haven't, you're probably him. This type of one-upmanship is particularly prevalent in backpacker circles. It's always about who stayed at the cheapest, dirtiest place, or who got invited to a local's abode to eat dubious delicacies off rustic instruments with questionable hygiene. Don't be the guy who needs to have the best story all the time; allow others to tell theirs too. It's a conversation, not an open-mic night.

Avoid asking the obvious: So what do you do? How do you know [mutual friend]? Where are you from?

I know it's tempting but people's jobs are probably not the most interesting thing about them. Personally, I start with a lighthearted comment or joke – usually about the host or someone we have in common. I was once in the kitchen of a Swedish hostel when another guest told his table-mates: "Someone just asked me what city I would live in if I had complete freedom to choose. What would be yours?" It was a quirky and interesting way to start a conversation. Failing that, offering your fellow travellers a drink, a snack or even a cigarette is sometimes the easiest way to win friends!

Show people that they've taught you something: If someone shares an interesting fact with you, demonstrate that they have taught you something.

Everyone loves to feel smart so people will warm to you immediately if they feel appreciated. Don't say, "Yes, I read that a few weeks ago" even if you have. Instead, make the other person feel interesting and knowledgeable. Once they are at ease, the conversation will flow more naturally and chances are they genuinely will teach you something interesting.

64. Let go of YOLO and FOMO

The phenomena of YOLO (You Only Live Once) and FOMO (Fear Of Missing Out) encourage us to say yes to everything. *'You're travelling'*, they say. *'Go out! Drink! Dance! Have fun!'*

Trying new things is important but if you want to avoid travel burnout, you must also learn to say no. You can't and won't see everything. You have a finite amount of time and a finite amount of energy so sometimes you'll have to miss out – not just on parties and events but sights and attractions too.

In Peru, we spent time in Lima, Cusco, Aguas Calientes for Machu Picchu, Nazca and Puno but we missed out on Colca Canyon and Chan Chan. In Argentina, we saw Ushuaia in Tierra del Fuego, El Calafate for Perito Moreno, El Chaltén and Buenos Aires but we missed Salta, Córdoba and Mendoza. Don't try to do everything. It's impossible and will leave you exhausted.

65. Accept the idea of single-serving friends

We shared a Tongan feast with Natasha and David on Tongatapu and a 20-mile walk with Mandy on 'Eua Island – and then never heard from them again. They had scribbled down our details but we failed to take theirs and they never got in touch. In other cases, it was the other way round. We learnt that that was okay.

Sure, you can add fellow travellers on Facebook and exchange occasional likes for the rest of your lives but it's also okay to spend a day or evening in really great company and then let them go. That's just the nature of travel.

66. Treat problems at source

Most experienced travellers advocate a relaxed attitude on the road. So what if your padlock needs to be jammed up and twisted to a 71.0007 degree angle and then pushed every time you need to open it? That's fine, they'll say. Chill.

And so what if your SD card doesn't quite work the first two times you stick it in your laptop? It's cool.

You've got another bout of Delhi Belly? Ride it out.

Taking a laissez-faire attitude to annoyances may be in keeping with the traveller's philosophy but dealing with the same issue again and again takes up more time in the long run. Get a new lock or an SD card, buy some decent medicine or go see a doctor.

Treating problems at source will free up your time and eliminate all the 'mini stresses' that can wear you down over time.

67. How to travel as a couple

Agree to outlaw one annoying habit: Most relationship experts will tell you to accept your partner with all their quirks and foibles. On the road, however, a 'quirk' can fester and grow into something unbearable. Perhaps one of you is more negative than the other, or one loves to shop and the other hates it. Identify one annoying habit each and agree to outlaw it.

Share the admin: Travel involves a great deal of research, planning, money management and interaction with others. Share the responsibility so that one person doesn't have to bear all the stress.

Don't play the blame game when a situation escalates: There's a horrifying film called Open Water in which two divers are mistakenly left stranded in the middle of the ocean by their dive company. They start off certain they will soon be collected. As the film progresses, their confidence gradually devolves to confusion, anxiety, panic and then hysteria. As their emotions escalate, the girl starts to blame her partner ("Why don't we stay with the group? We always have to do things different than everybody else" and "*I* wanted to go skiing.")

The blame game plays to a similar tune. You miss a train or boat and initially it's fine and you laugh about it. And then it gets dark and cold and you're tired and hungry so you start hinting that it's the other person's fault. Eventually, you end up bickering and then arguing.

Don't start the blame game just because a situation worsens. Even if it is the other person's fault, you were fine about it five hours ago; it's not suddenly more their fault just because things got worse.

Spend time apart: We met a couple in Tonga who would occasionally spend a day away from each other. If they had three days in Buenos Aires, for example, they would spend the third day doing their own thing.

We didn't try this but we did spend a day apart in San Francisco when I (Kia) was meeting friends of mine and Peter was hanging out with our hosts, old friends from London. When we met again in the evening, we both realised that we hadn't been apart for a whole day in about six months. It was a strange feeling and made us appreciate being together again.

Don't forego date night: About once a month, Peter and I put aside our walking boots, put on the cleanest things in our backpacks and went to a restaurant slightly above our budget. This was less important in the South Pacific because it was so naturally beautiful. In South America, however, it was a nice way to escape the noise, dust and traffic. Don't let your constant proximity mask the fact that you need some quality downtime together.

Be mindful of mutual money: Every couple has a different attitude to money. In London, Peter and I keep separate finances so we never pay attention to each other's spending. On the road, however, we spend from one pot. As such, we have to be mindful that we're spending mutual money.

Peter buys a coffee most mornings whereas I don't drink coffee so we joke that I have a 'coffee fund' with which I can buy small (usually chocolate-based) treats. Thankfully, our discrepancies aren't that pronounced. No couple wants to count pennies but if you're having five beers to your partner's one coke every evening, you may need to rein in the spending and be more mindful that you're spending their money too.

Learn your partner's fight style: When Peter is angry, you'll know it. He shouts and swears and gesticulates more than an Italian gangster. I on the other hand will sulk for about 20 minutes after which I'll usually be over it. In the early days, Peter used to try to coax me out of my sulks, consequently becoming frustrated at my unresponsiveness. He has since learnt that he just needs to leave me alone; to not ask me any questions or make any demands; to let me process my anger and return to rational action. Conversely, I know that when he's shouting, I need to let him shout.

If you learn the other person's fight style, you'll find that arguments pass more quickly. In addition, plan for your triggers. If you get irritable when you're hungry, pack a snack. If you get snippy when you're cold, pack a fleece.

Act with kindness: I hate to come over all Awaken the Giant Within but this last point is worth mentioning as it's the most sensible thing I've read about relationships.

In her 2014 article Masters of Love, Emily Esfahani Smith looks at scientific research on what keeps couples together. The short answer is kindness – an admittedly nebulous term. We can try to define what constitutes kindness using Smith's example. Let's say your partner has received the excellent news that she got into medical school. She may say something like "I got into my top choice med school!" You then have four choices in how you react:

- **Active constructive:** engaging wholeheartedly ("That's great! Congratulations! When did you find out?")
- **Passive constructive:** reacting in a half-hearted, understated way ("That's great, babe")
- **Passive destructive:** ignoring the event or changing the subject ("Cool, I've just won some Amazon vouchers")
- **Active destructive:** actively diminishing good news ("Are you sure you can handle all the studying? And what about the cost? Med school is so expensive.")

This doesn't just apply to big news either. To use another of Smiths' examples, say a bird enthusiast notices a goldfinch fly across his yard. He might say to his wife, "Look at that beautiful bird outside!" (what psychologist John Gottman calls a 'bid' for contact). She can choose to put down her book and have a look (active constructive), give him a passive constructive "That's nice", ignore him altogether or say something actively destructive like "Stop interrupting me, I'm reading." It may sound trivial but research shows that partners who answer bids positively are the ones with the healthiest and longest lasting relationships.

68. Be humble

Ok, so you might be traversing hostile deserts and discovering new species but must you bore your friends to distraction with it?

Posting several times a day on Facebook about yet another amazing sunset over the Indian Ocean or your daring trek through Jericho last night might elicit a few fittingly envious comments but soon enough, you'll start being X'd from people's newsfeeds. You won't know of course so it may be no skin off your nose, but if you want some friends left on your return, go easy on the bragging.

Instead, set up a dedicated space (a blog, an Instagram account) so if people really want to keep up to date with your travels, they can proactively seek out the details instead of having it all shoved down their throats.

CHAPTER 10: HEALTH

69. Always wear sunscreen

If you find yourself asking "do I need sunscreen?", the answer is yes. It's always yes.

Our travels exposed us to extremely strong rays and we weren't always appropriately protected. I'm browner than Peter and don't burn easily so I became complacent on the road. Over the course of the trip, the skin on my legs became dry, cracked and lost its smoothness. Even a year after returning home, I could still tell the difference – an issue I could have avoided with just a touch more diligence.

Sun damage doesn't happen overnight which breeds complacency but it does catch up with you, so be a stickler.

70. Leave enough time for jabs

In preparation for our trip around the world, we had jabs for Tetanus, Typhoid, Hepatitis A, Hepatitis B, Yellow Fever and Rabies, as well as tablets for Malaria.

You will likely need a similarly comprehensive course of vaccinations for your trip around the world. Some of these will need to be administered in stages and may take a month or so to kick in. As such, visit your doctor two months before your planned departure date to find out what you need and to agree a schedule. See fitfortravel.nhs.uk/destinations.aspx for an idea of what you may need.

As mentioned in tip 14. Document your jabs, carry a digital and physical record of your vaccinations as you may need to show proof that you have them before entering certain countries. The record will also come in use for future reference.

As noted in tip 1. Use the budget formula, vaccinations can cost a great deal so make sure you factor in the fees.

71. Use a water purifier

We've stayed in some pretty basic places during the course of our travels. There was the Fijian campsite in Taveuni with rather sketchy facilities, the Samoan beach fale in Savai'i which didn't have walls, and the Colombian campsite in San Agustin with drinking water that ran a brownish yellow. In all these places, we were able to drink the tap water (hose water in one case) because we were able to purify water on the go.

In our past travels to India, Bangladesh, Tanzania, Cambodia and the like, we've tried purifying filters, tablets, iodine, chlorine and good old-fashioned boiling, but these have either been ineffectual, impractical or just tasted awful. For this reason, we have settled on the SteriPEN Ultra (steripen.com/ultra).

We like it because:

It's super quick: Unlike boiling water (and water filters), the SteriPEN is quick. It takes a mere 90 seconds to sterilise one litre of water and 50 seconds for half a litre.

It's portable: At 140g, the SteriPEN weighs less than a bottle of water. It fits down the side of a backpack, in a wash bag or even a handbag.

It can be charged by USB: The bane of any backpacker travelling with gadgets is the numerous different chargers.

The SteriPEN can be charged by USB meaning you just need to carry a cable to charge it (via mains, a solar charger or a laptop). One full charge lasts 50 uses.

It has no effect on taste: Unlike chlorine and iodine, the SteriPEN has no effect on taste, meaning delicious water will remain delicious and, unfortunately, awful water will taste awful. Perhaps if they introduced a strawberry infusion, it'd be perfect.

It's value for money: So, what's the catch? Well, at $99, it's not easy on the pocket. If you're a frequent or long-term traveller, however, it will cost you less than buying bottled water all the time. For us, the comparison was $99 versus about $365 worth of bottled water (each) over the course of a year. The SteriPEN lasts 8,000 uses – a lot cheaper than 8,000 bottles of water!

72. How to deal with tummy bugs

We were lucky enough to avoid stomach upsets through 40 countries of travel... and then Kia swallowed a mouthful of water in a swimming pool in Egypt.

However strong your constitution, a tummy bug is inevitable at some point in your travel life. You can, however, reduce the risk by following these steps.

- Purify tap water (see tip 71) or stick to bottled water
- Avoid ice in your drinks if the source is unclear
- Opt for fruit that can be peeled (e.g. bananas, oranges)
- Be discerning with street food vendors and avoid anything that looks unclean
- Carry antibacterial gel or wet wipes to clean your hands where soap and water are unavailable
- Carry some anti-diarrhea pills (e.g. Imodium) in your hand luggage at all times

If the worst happens, book yourself into a comfortable hostel or hotel, take some Imodium and drink plenty of water to keep hydrated. While recovering, stick to non-spiced foods like rice for a day or two.

If conditions don't improve, seek advice at a local pharmacy.

73. Watch your snacking

When on the road (especially when travelling solo), it can be tempting to grab a doughnut in the morning and then a mid-morning coffee and then a mid-afternoon crepe and of course a nightcap before retiring for the day. Stopping for snacks is a great way to break up the day but try not to overdo it.

Long journeys are a particular danger zone. It's easy to sit there dipping into an oversized bag of potato chips while watching the scenery unfold through the window, but try to refrain. Travelling is meant to be indulgent of course but don't go overboard. It's not good for your health and you'll feel worse for it.

74. Prepare for female backpacker problems

Let's be honest, men and women aren't quite 'equal' on the road. We women have to deal with periods, public toilet seats and keeping up appearances. Here's how to deal with some common female backpacker problems.

Getting your period on the road: Even Bodyform – who peddled the idea of the miniskirted, roller-skating, skydiving girl-on-period for years – admitted in 2012 that they were lying. In truth, periods can be a pain especially if you're planning an active trip. There are several ways you can control your period: contraceptive pills which you can use for three months in a row without a break, an IUD or a contraceptive injection. Naturally, you should get medical advice before using any of these methods. If you still plan to have your period, consider switching from tampons to a menstrual cup which female Atlas & Boots readers swear by. (If you're still using towels, for the love of God, switch to tampons!)

Public toilet seats: I trialled the Sheewee (the 'female urination device') but found it cumbersome and unhygienic, so went back to arranging tissue across a toilet seat with the attention and care of a bomb disposal expert. Some women, however, sing the Sheewee's praises so it's worth a try. Consider pairing it with a Peebol, a packet full of rapid performing absorbent granules that convert fluid into a biodegradable gel. This allows you to relieve yourself when you don't have access to a bathroom.

Unwanted hair: One of my life's greatest regrets is not being born with the type of hair that can be coaxed into the voluptuous tresses you see in adverts and on catwalks. It's just too fine. The only benefit is that it's fine everywhere else, which means I can go a couple of weeks without shaving my legs. Even so, unwanted hair is still a problem.

There are several options available but all have their pros and cons: professional waxing lasts longer but is an expensive habit; home waxing is cheaper but less reliable when using untested products; shaving offers a great finish but doesn't last long. My solution was to pack an epilator which was long lasting and effective with no recurring cost.

Keeping up appearances: Research shows that the majority of women spend about an hour on their appearance every day. In a self-inflicted 'tax' of sorts, we check our reflections more often than men, spend more time adjusting our composure and body language, and fret more about the shape of our bodies. Despite the idea of the carefree female backpacker who's more concerned with experiences than appearances, the truth is that many of us do worry about the way we look. In fact, when Peter asked if he could post a video of me atop Nevis Peak in St Kitts & Nevis, my response wasn't "Sure, I worked bloody hard to get up there!" but "Nooo, I look awful."

My solution on the road was to focus on getting healthy rather than getting pretty: healthy hair, healthy skin, and healthy body. I focused on long-term solutions that negated the need for a glut of makeup: vitamins, exercise and nourishing oils for my hair and skin. My favourite products are Estee Lauder Advanced Night Repair Cream, Paula's Choice Liquid Exfoliant, Viviscal, Floradix and plenty of sunscreen!

75. Understand heat exhaustion

It's important to differentiate between **heat exhaustion** and **heat stroke.** Heat exhaustion is when your body becomes very hot and starts to lose water or salt. Heat stroke is when your body can no longer cool itself and its temperature becomes dangerously high (104°F / 40°C or higher). It may be referred to as 'sunstroke' when the symptoms are caused by prolonged exposure to sunlight.

Heat stroke is less common but more serious. It's important to be able to recognise both conditions, especially as heat exhaustion can lead to heat stroke if left untreated.

Recognise heat exhaustion

Heat exhaustion symptoms

- Intense thirst
- Feeling weak and tired
- Feeling faint or dizzy
- Throbbing headache
- Nausea and vomiting
- Muscle cramps
- Profuse sweating
- Flushed skin
- Rapid heartbeat
- Urinating less often and having much darker urine than usual

Heat stroke symptoms

- Confusion
- Disorientation
- Seizure
- Loss of consciousness

Treat heat exhaustion

Rest in a cool place: Find shade and rest for at least 30 minutes. Lie down if possible. If your symptoms are severe, consider waiting until the sun is lower in the sky before resuming activity. Naturally, you should make sure there is enough daylight to safely end the hike.

Remove excess clothing: Take off any tight or heavy clothing to allow air to circulate around your body.

Cool your skin: Use a wet buff or cloth, or a cold pack to cool your neck and armpits. Fan your wet skin to cool it.

Rehydrate: Drink plenty of water, fruit juice or a rehydration drink if available. This will replenish lost water and salt.

Know when to call for help: If you feel confused or disoriented, call for medical help. If a hiking companion falls unconscious, follow the steps above and place the person in recovery position until help arrives. If they have a seizure, remove any rocks or objects near to them to prevent injury.

Avoid heat exhaustion

Acclimatise: If you are hiking away from home in hotter temperatures than what you're used to, it will take you time to acclimatise to the heat. Wait a few days before attempting any vigorous activity, especially a long or strenuous hike.

Check for heatwave warnings: Make sure you read the weather forecast for the day(s) of your hike. It's easy to ignore this in countries with seemingly endless good weather but heatwaves can be just as dangerous as storms, so don't get complacent.

Factor in rest time: A six-hour hike may not be a six-hour hike in extremely high temperatures. Factor in plenty of rest time. This way, you will be under less pressure to maintain a strenuous pace. Take frequent breaks in the shade and check on your companions.

Avoid sunburn: Sunburn reduces your body's ability to rid itself of heat. As such, make absolute sure that you apply and re-apply sunscreen of at least SPF 15 throughout your hike.

Wear light clothing: Loose-fitting, lightweight and light-coloured clothing are best for hot hiking. They will reflect heat, allow air to circulate and enable sweat evaporation. Avoid tight, heavy and dark clothing for they will do the exact opposite!

Drink plenty of water: Some experts say you should drink more than you need while others claim you should only drink when you're thirsty. A good rule of thumb is to drink at least three litres of water over the course of the day; four if the hike is strenuous. Drink 750ml two hours before and another 250ml when you start. Drink the rest at frequent intervals over the course of the day.

Splash water over your skin: In very hot weather, it's useful to sprinkle water over your skin or clothes. A wet buff around your neck will help keep you cool.

Cover the basics: Whether hot hiking, night hiking or endurance hiking, make sure you pack the '10 essential systems' (see the starred items in Appendix A: Packing List). This equipment list has been developed by experts over the years and will help you stay safe in case your plans go awry.

76. Understand altitude sickness

Altitude sickness occurs when your body can't get enough oxygen from the air at altitude. It most commonly happens when people go quickly from low altitude to 2,400m or above (about 8,000ft). Symptoms usually surface between six and 24 hours after ascending and are often worse at night. Here's what to look out for.

Recognise altitude sickness

Common altitude sickness symptoms

- Throbbing headache
- Loss of appetite
- Feeling weak, tired or dizzy
- Nausea and vomiting
- Upset stomach
- Difficulty sleeping
- Shortness of breath
- Increased heart rate

Serious altitude sickness symptoms

Altitude sickness can affect your lungs and brain, which is very serious. When this happens, symptoms can include:

- Feeling confused
- Feeling faint or drowsy
- Clumsiness or difficulty walking
- Irrational behaviour
- Breathlessness when resting
- Bubbling sound in the chest when breathing
- A persistent, irritable cough (you may cough up pink or white frothy liquid)

- Blue or grey lips or fingernails
- Double vision
- Convulsions

Treat altitude sickness

Go low: If you experience severe symptoms, you must immediately get to a lower altitude (at least 450m / 1,500ft) and seek emergency help. Always take someone with you and never let someone else with severe symptoms descend alone.

Get more oxygen: If you're on a particularly challenging climb, your guide or group may have access to oxygen or a specially designed pressure chamber to treat altitude sickness.

Rest: Limit any walking or activity. Stop any exercise and take it easy. Be honest with your guide or group about how you're feeling. If you ascend further, your symptoms may become severe in which case you can't just 'wait it out'.

Drink plenty of water: Keep hydrated by drinking plenty of fluids but stay away from alcohol. And, of course, don't smoke.

Treat your headache: You may take over-the-counter medicine such as ibuprofen (Advil, Nurofen) or paracetamol to treat your headache.

Consider altitude sickness tablets: Some climbers choose to take acetazolamide (Diamox) to speed up how fast their bodies get used to altitude. It's worth noting, however, the drug isn't licensed in some countries including the UK.

Avoid altitude sickness

Avoid flying into high-altitude cities: If you can, avoid flying straight into high-altitude cities like Lhasa in China.

Acclimatise: If you are climbing higher than 2,400m (8,000ft), spend at least one night at medium altitude before climbing higher.

Sleep low: Sleep at an altitude lower than where you were during the day. "Climb high, sleep low" is standard practice for those who spend time at high altitudes.

Ascend slowly: Once you're above 3,000m (10,000ft), don't increase the altitude at which you sleep by more than 500m a night. You can climb higher during the day, but should come back to a camp no more than 500m above the night before.

Amend your diet: Avoid heavy meals before reaching altitude but once there, eat a high-calorie diet that includes a lot of carbs such as bread, cereal and pasta. (Yay, altitude!) Drink plenty of water and avoid smoking and alcohol.

Use sunscreen and sunglasses: To protect your overall wellbeing at altitude, make sure you use extra sunscreen and pack sunglasses or goggles to protect against snow blindness.

CHAPTER 11: PHOTOGRAPHY

77. Keep your photos safe

When we returned from travelling, I (Peter) had a heart-stopping moment where I thought I had erased the iPhoto library containing photos from our last three months on the road – including the stunning Perito Moreno in Argentina and Iguassu Falls in Brazil.

To my eternal relief, it was a false alarm but it certainly curbed my complacency. I now use a multi-step backup system to keep my memories safe. If your photos are important, it's prudent that you do the same.

Cloud services: In the past I've used services such as Dropbox or Google Drive but they rely on manual backup across different formats and are space restricted. Eyefi Cloud automatically updates from Eyefi's app on either your computer or smartphone and has unlimited storage – useful when dealing with large numbers of RAW resolution photos and videos. The cloud service can also send optimised versions of your files back to your mobile devices, so you don't take up too much storage space on your smartphone.

External hard drives: If you've just finished the trip of a lifetime, it's worth backing up your files onto external hard drives as well. At home I have a pair of durable Western Digital My Books with fast FireWire connections for all of my documents and photography. It may also be worth considering fireproof and waterproof external hard drives if you have particularly sensitive files or documents that need securing. I use Time Machine on Apple OSX to back up automatically and periodically.

On the road, I need something more lightweight and therefore carry a Transcend Storejet 2TB hard drive which is small and portable, and comes with built-in power saving making it ideal for outdoor and adventure travel.

Manual backup: This is the most time-consuming method and a little "old school" but it's worth considering if you want a third layer of security. DVDs are the safest format to use and can be easily and securely stored away in binders. You can also make copies and leave them with friends and family. Naturally, this should be coupled with an external or online backup that happens in real time. Otherwise, optical media will by default leave you with periods of time where files have not yet been backed up.

Wifi SD cards: I recently invested in some Eyefi SD cards to ensure I never lose a photograph again. Eyefi's Mobi Pro SD cards have built-in wifi which offers automatic backup across different media. The original file remains on your SD card but copies of your files can be automatically sent via wifi to your computer, hard drives, mobile devices and a cloud service. It means that even if you forget to back up at the end of a day's shooting, your images will be safely copied to your devices.

One is never enough: I can't stress enough how important it is to use more than one of the above photo backup methods. Hardware can break, connections get interrupted, software crashes or we forget to click the burn button. Whichever you choose, it's important to make your backup procedures regular and stick to them religiously. If you let it slip, it will come back to bite you. Trust me.

Extra tips:

- When using photo-editing software, don't edit the originals. Save them in a separate library.
- If something fails – like an SD card or hard drive – stop using it immediately. It will be easier for data recovery software to find lost files.
- Remove SD cards, drives and devices safely.
- Don't completely fill storage devices (including SD cards) – leave some space on them.
- To preserve SD cards, delete photos on your computer, not your camera.
- Periodically reformat SD cards on the camera.
- Replace/recharge batteries before they drain completely.
- Store a locked photo of your name and contact details on your memory cards in case you lose them.

78. How to take better photos

Know the basics: To make the switch from auto to manual you need to know the basics of shutter speed, aperture and ISO settings. Below are the bare minimum basics depending on what you're shooting. These are not hard and fast rules, but they were enough to get me (Peter) started.

- Large aperture for depth (portraits and close-ups)
- Small aperture for landscapes and wide shots
- Fast shutter speed for action and movement (waterfalls, animals, sports)
- Slow shutter speed for low light level (tripod is often required)
- Large aperture and fast shutter speed for shots with depth
- Small aperture and slow shutter speed for flat shots
- ISO controls the sensor/light sensitivity – this can mean

trading quality for exposure

- Learn the Sunny f16 rule – old school but still relevant

Get out of auto: Every photographer is guilty of auto sometimes – myself included. Switching to manual gives you a greater degree of control over the camera, particularly depth and focus. Simply put, Full Auto mode will mostly try to use shutter speed between 1/100 and 1/200 and a mid-range aperture like f10-f12. When these are viewed at 100%, softness will likely be revealed, compromising quality. In good light, shutter speeds should really be much higher.

Think about composition: Composing your shot is half the work, particularly with landscape and travel photography. I learnt the following rules years ago when I was a student and they still serve me well during shooting as well as post-production.

Rule of thirds: In its basic form, split the shot into thirds vertically and horizontally, and try to divide up the shot. This is particularly useful with shots of horizons. Also, think about where the 'action' in a shot will be unfolding. On the intersection of two points is usually a good place.

Perspective and depth of field: Photographs always become more interesting when there is depth involved – just like art. Using manual camera settings will help you partially achieve this, but composing your shot carefully before you snap will greatly improve the outcome.

Use of lines and frames: Use naturally occurring lines and frames to lead the viewer to what you want them to focus on. Lines can help give a photograph depth and perspective. Frames can enclose a shot, giving it a natural frame.

Use AF point selection: Decide where in the frame you want to focus. On most modern cameras you have a choice of at least eight different focus points as well as the central AF point used in auto mode. You should tell the camera where to focus, not the other way around. This will help you develop all of the aforementioned skills, particularly when working with depth.

Create some presets: Fiddling around with buttons in manual mode when a once-in-a-lifetime shot is unfolding in front of you only to get the wrong shutter speed and end up with nothing but a frame of white or black is deeply frustrating. You'll be left thinking that you should have stuck to auto mode! Create some presets that you know work in certain environments. Most digital SLRs will allow at least three.

Some quick fixes:

- Carry a lightweight mini-tripod or spider for low-level lighting and timer shots.
- Move! Don't be afraid to get "down and dirty" to get the best shots. My teacher forced me to use a fixed lens when I was learning.
- Know how to clean your sensor. Cameras differ but, in general, remove the lens and switch to bulb so you can control how long the shutter stays open. Then, use a cotton bud to clear any dirt and dust that has made its way in.
- Buy a telephoto lens for getting that shot when you simply can't get close enough. Think safaris and crowded markets.

79. How to photograph locals

How is it that some photographers seem to get under the skin of a community and come away with such stunning photos? We spoke to a number of experts to find out.

Don't observe – participate: "Get outside of your comfort zone and participate in a local experience that involves people," advises culture photographer Oded Wagenstein. "On the most basic level, it is much easier to shoot portraits of market stall owners if you buy something from them. Swap the hotel room for a homestay or eat local street food. By being a participant, you can shoot better portraits in a way that is much more fun and meaningful than just stopping someone on the street."

Learn some of the local language: "Knowing another language is one of the most important skills you can develop as a traveller," says documentary photographer Nick St. Oegger. "It will only open more doors for you, allowing you to communicate with people you wouldn't otherwise be able to. Even if you just pick up the basics of the language in the country you are visiting, the local people will usually open up to you."

Be respectful – of their time and their customs: "When photographing local people, speed is a crucial component," says portrait photographer Marcel Kolacek. "Never make people wait several minutes. Even a minute is a very long time for a person who you just met. It's also important to be aware of local customs. An integral part is respect, good manners, tolerance and the ability to conform to local conditions."

Travel alone: Travelling by yourself is a great way to endear yourself to locals and to open up lines of communication. Photographer Lexi Novitske says: "People open up to me much more as a single traveller. They invite me into their homes, push their babies into my arms, and bond over curiosity in my cultural differences. Being alone also helps because you're able to have a lot more time to interact with the subjects without pressure."

Hand over your camera: "There are situations where people are distrustful of cameras," warns Lexi. "Sometimes it's a spiritual belief that the camera steals a piece of their soul, or wariness that their photo will be used against them. Yet, there is always a kid that's curious about the camera and eager to start taking shots of his family and friends. Once a few gather around to see the images, others often ask for photos to be taken of them as well."

Don't fear rejection: Sometimes people don't want to have their photograph taken. Depending on local conditions, circumstances and an individual's mood you may well get rejected. It's no bad thing and you shouldn't let it daunt you. Thank them and put away your camera. Someone who feels uncomfortable having his or her photograph taken probably wouldn't make a good subject anyway.

Don't overthink: "Good portrait photography often happens spontaneously," says photojournalist Janet Kotwas. "If you see that once-in-a-lifetime image, take it! Try not to overthink or over-manipulate the scene. You may miss the moment and imperfections can be beautiful. If you're looking for something special, try new angles – get low, shoot from above, get close to fill your frame. Let the story unfold naturally, then capture the moment uniquely; how you see it through your lens, differently to everyone else."

Decide where you stand on paying: Taking the above steps will make photographing local people much easier but there's always a chance you will be asked to pay some money for the privilege. The ethics around this is a point of debate.

In terms of our view, when we had a chance to photograph a young girl on the Uros Islands in Peru in exchange for a few sols, we declined. Treating her as a commodity felt distasteful but was this just western paternalism at play? Deciding where you stand will make in-the-moment interactions easier. Whatever your view, it's a good idea to keep some loose change on you in case someone asks for money retrospectively (i.e. after agreeing to and posing for a photo).

CHAPTER 12: LANGUAGE

80. Ignore language learning myths

Language learning is subjective. Some people seem to have a natural talent for it while others find it near impossible. With the right level of dedication, however, any average learner can pick up a new language.

We examine five language myths below to make sure you're best equipped for your journey to fluency.

Myth 1. You're too old to learn a new language

One of the things we hear most often is that children learn language faster than adults. This is usually rooted in the 'critical period hypothesis' which suggests that children are better at learning languages because their brains are more elastic [1]. However, since its inception, this theory has been repeatedly questioned [2] and experimental research has shown that adolescents and adults perform better than young children under controlled conditions [3]. In addition, it's also a myth that younger children learn languages quicker than older ones [4]. In short: you're not too old to learn a new language so don't use that as an excuse.

Myth 2. The best way to learn is to live in a foreign country

Conventional wisdom dictates that if you want to learn Spanish, you should move to Spain. This sounds like a great idea, but moving to a new country without learning some grammar first will force you to pick up bad habits. You may think you'll improve with time, but consider how many first-generation immigrants use phrases like "I take it" instead of "I will take it" despite being in the country for more than a decade. Moving to a new country is not a surefire way to learn a new language. You may be better off practising at home first where you have the time and luxury to learn proper grammar and sentence structure first.

Myth 3. If you listen to a language every day, you'll learn it by osmosis

There can be a temptation to put on a local language radio channel and hope that some of it enters your consciousness without effort, but effective language learning involves *all* forms of learning: reading, writing, listening and speaking. Passive learning will certainly help your accent and pronunciation but research shows that it's insufficient by itself as a way to learn a new language.

Myth 4. Pronunciation doesn't need active work

Pronunciation is the most neglected area of language learning. Test your verbal skills on real native speakers outside of a classroom setting and aim for a near-native pronunciation – this is where local language radio, TV and film will help.

Myth 5. You shouldn't worry about making mistakes

As children, we are often prompted to interact in class with promises that it's okay to make mistakes. In language learning, however, mistakes can be harmful. Each time you use improper grammar, you increase the chances of you making the same mistake again. Some learners will want to learn as much as possible as quickly as possible but there is a big difference between fluency *with mistakes* and fluency *without mistakes* and it's far harder to jump from the first to the second than building the second from the ground up. Take the time to learn the grammar and to structure proper sentences. It will be slow going, but it's the only way to do it if you want to be truly fluent.

[1] Lenneberg, 1967; Penfield & Roberts, 1959
[2] Geneses, 1981; Harley, 1989; Newport, 1990
[3] Snow & Hoefnagel-Hoehle, 1978
[4] Stern, Burstall, & Harley, 1975; Gorosch & Axelsson, 1964; Buehler, 1972; Florander & Jansen, 1968

81. What's the best language to learn?

The 'best' language to learn depends on your aims and motivations. Below, we take a look at the best language to learn based on different criteria.

Most widely spoken

1. Mandarin: 955m speakers
2. Spanish: 405m
3. English: 360m
4. Hindi: 310m
5. Arabic: 295m

(Source: Nationalencyklopedin 2010 estimates)

Most 'widely' spoken is a common deciding factor but it's also a bit of a misnomer. If you learn Chinese, you can speak to 37% of the world's total population but only three countries count Mandarin as a national language. In contrast, French is a national language in approximately 29 countries across the world. Unless you plan to spend a substantial amount of time in China and its rural areas, this reason can be a bit of a red herring.

Best for business

1. English (US: 17,968 GDP and UK: 3,039 GDP)
2. Mandarin (China: 11,385)
3. Japanese (Japan: 4,116)
4. German (Germany: 3,325)
5. French (France: 2,418)

(Source: World Economic League Table 2016)

Another popular criterion for choosing a language is the potential career benefits it might offer. The rationale is that if you can converse in the language of the world's strongest economies, you'll be in better stead for employment and progression. Under this criterion, Mandarin is once again the best language to learn as an English speaker. However, it's worth noting that due to its complexity, Mandarin is unlikely to become the standard language for business.

Ease of learning

1. Spanish
2. Portuguese
3. French
4. Italian
5. Romanian
6. Dutch
7. Swedish
8. Afrikaans
9. Norwegian

(Source: FSI, US Department of State)

If you want to learn a language purely for academic reasons (i.e. to exercise your learning muscles or just as a hobby), then level of ease is a perfectly acceptable way to choose. According to the Foreign Service Institute of the US Department of State, English speakers can relatively easily pick up eight European languages as well as Afrikaans (with 600 class hours per language that is).

Beauty

1. French
2. Spanish
3. Italian
4. Portuguese
5. Romanian

Alas, there is no way to subjectively measure the beauty of languages. However, if you're set on becoming a modern-day Don Juan, few would argue against the Romance languages listed above. French in particular is, as a character from The Matrix put it, like wiping your arse with silk. Can't argue with that.

Culture

Finally, we come to what is probably the best criterion for choosing what language you want to learn. Which country or countries do you see yourself spending time in? How much do you like the locals? What literature do you wish you could read in its original language? What films do you wish you could understand? If you have a genuine interest and passion for a language and the culture behind it, you will more likely persevere when you hit a wall.

The verdict

If we were to take a completely objective point of view, we would recommend French. It ticks all the boxes. It may not be the most 'widely spoken' language by volume but its reach goes much further than Mandarin and its economy is only behind China, Japan and Germany in terms of non-English speaking countries. Furthermore, French is relatively easy, sounds beautiful and has a rich and colourful culture to boot. Overall, we recommend French.

82. Learn some vocabulary tricks

After five months in South America followed by several months of self-study, I (Kia) finally got a handle on Spanish grammar. I then shifted focus onto vocabulary which is much more fun. Below are six ways in which I improved my vocabulary.

Gather a list of cognates: In linguistics, a cognate is a word that is very similar to another. There are hundreds of cognates shared by English and the Romance languages (Spanish, Portuguese, French, Italian, and Romanian). Many of these are 'perfect cognates' (i.e. words that are spelled exactly the same and which have the same meaning) while many others are near perfect.

English to Spanish perfect cognates

- Animal – Animal
- Capital – Capital
- Cultural – Cultural
- Director – Director
- Doctor – Doctor

English to Spanish near-perfect cognates

- Attention – Atención
- Celebration – Celebración
- Dramatic – Dramático
- Perfect – Perfecto
- Secretary – Secretario

Gathering a comprehensive list of cognates will demonstrate just how much vocabulary you already know – before you've even started studying! As a first step, search in Google for 'English [Spanish] cognates', replacing 'Spanish' for the language of your choice. Save these in a flashcard app like Quizlet (quizlet.com).

Don't worry if you're not learning a Romance language. Many other languages including Russian, Japanese and Bengali have 'loaned' words from English and integrated them into their vocabulary, so it's likely you will already know some words despite the different script.

Tip: Check the meaning of cognates you encounter in everyday reading before adding them to your list as they could be false friends (i.e. words that sound alike but do not mean the same thing). For example, embarazado in Spanish does not mean 'embarrassed' as one might suspect, but pregnant!

Translate the '300 instant sight words': Dr Edward Fry, author of 1000 Instant Words, found in 1996 that a mere 300 words make up approximately 65% of all written material in English. Download his list of 300 instant sight words (atlasandboots.com/files/fry.pdf) and work on translating the words to the language you're learning. Store the translations in Quizlet and revisit them regularly. This won't mean you will understand 65% of all written material in your new language (you need grammar for that!), but it *will* give you a great start. You may wish to sort them into verbs, nouns, prepositions and so on to help your learning.

Use word association: Learning by rote isn't always effective in language learning. Sometimes, you need to use shortcuts or tricks to remember specific words. This is where word association comes in.

First, think of what the foreign word reminds you of. What do the syllables sound like? What do they call to mind? Then, try to bridge that to the meaning of the word. For example, the Spanish word sacar means to take out. 'Sacar' sounds like 'sack' and 'car' so if you imagine taking out a sack of rubbish from your car, it may help you remember that sacar means to take out.

Learn phrases; not just words: Our native languages are so easy because we recognise not just words but hundreds of common phrases too. We process these as a single entity rather than individual words. They range from prosaic phrases such as 'how are you?' and 'I'm very well' to more colourful ones like 'an axe to grind' and 'at the crack of dawn'. Learning phrases has two advantages: first, it adds context to words that may be otherwise difficult to remember and, second, it allows you to recognise blocks of words, making overall comprehension more fluid.

Use virtual immersion: The best way to improve your vocabulary is to immerse yourself in the language you are learning. It won't always be possible to do this physically in which case you have to rely on virtual immersion. Try the below sites.

- **Listen:** Visit TuneIn (tunein.com) to find radio stations in the language of your choice.
- **Read:** Use Alexa (alexa.com/topsites/countries) to identify top sites in the language/region of your choice. You may have to filter out all the search engines and social sites, but it will give you an idea of interesting content sites.
- **Watch:** Use Yabla (yabla.com) to watch videos in the language of your choice. Foreign language films are also a great way to improve your vocabulary. Simply search in Google for 'IMDb: Highest Rated X-Language Feature Films' where 'X' is replaced by your language of choice.
- **Speak:** Visit italki (italki.com) to find foreign language tutors for as little as $5 an hour. Additionally, consider joining a local meetup group.

Naturally, it's important to dedicate time to proactive study too. We recommend Duolingo (duolingo.com) and regular drills with Quizlet (quizlet.com).

Interrogate difficult words: When you're starting out, it's okay to skip over words you don't understand but once you reach level B1 in the Common European Framework of Reference for Languages, it's good practice to interrogate these further.

For example, when reading and translating an article on BBC World, I came across the word 'embargadora' for which I failed to find a translation in even stem or infinitive form. As a beginner, I would have let this go but instead I asked for a translation on Q&A site Quora and received some helpful responses. Granted, we will seldom use words we can't even find in the dictionary but isn't discovering new words part of the reason we're learning a language in the first place?

83. Tips for learning multiple languages

We spoke to a number of polyglots and multilinguals to see how they acquired their numerous languages. They shared a wealth of information, the best of which we share below.

Note: 'First language' is used to denote the first foreign language you have chosen to learn, not your mother tongue.

Don't give up on your first choice: Most people choose their first language for a reason. This may be via a systematic review of the best language to learn, a desire to speak with locals while travelling, or an interest in a specific foreign culture. Giving up on your first language sets a precedence, making it easier to quit subsequent efforts.

"Instead of quitting, find what works for you," says London-based Kiyeun Baek who speaks English, Spanish, Korean, Japanese and French, some daily in her role as head of business development at global publisher DK. "For me, it's starting to read real novels in the language as soon as possible."

Polyglot Judith Meyer speaks nine languages (with another four at beginner or intermediate level). She advises: "Try a different method or different materials first. If you're bored with a course or you can't understand it, just do something else for a while: a different course or even some fun activities like surfing the web or watching funny videos."

Judith advises native English speakers to choose a European language first before advancing to more difficult languages further afield: "Any European language is an okay first choice and it doesn't make much sense to switch – for example, from French to Spanish – when you run into trouble because you'll lose your progress only to encounter the exact same difficulties again."

Understand the components of 'natural talent': Our experts agree that motivation is the most important ingredient in learning multiple languages. Interestingly, they urge us to interrogate the notion of 'natural talent'. Rather than a singular trait that some people have and some don't, natural talent can be broken down into components.

Judith says: "I think there are talents for various aspects that are important in language learning. For example, there are people who have the gift of imitating accents: they hear very well and they are able to reproduce sounds more faithfully than the rest of us. There are people who have particularly good memory skills. Daniel Tammet, who made the news for learning Icelandic in a week, formerly placed fourth in the World Memory Championships. [His memory] definitely helped. Synaesthesia also helps. However, I don't believe in a separate language gene."

Framing natural talent in this way makes it less daunting. In lieu of a great memory, you might be good at talking to people and picking up language that way. Equally, you may not be great with grammar but your accent might be perfect.

Layer your learning by following the 70/30 rule: One question asked by every aspiring polyglot is: should I learn my languages in parallel or in sequence? Our considered answer is neither.

Lora Green from 2Polyglot (2polyglot.com) speaks four languages and explains: "Don't start learning two languages at once because all rules and definitions will be mixed in your mind, but don't wait until you speak one language fluently before taking courses in the second because there's no strict line where you can tell you speak a language fluently. You will just waste time. When you can express your opinion, understand grammar basics and follow what's going on in a TV series in your first language, use this as a sign that you may start learning another one."

Lora adds: "I use a proportion of 70/30. I use 70% of my language learning time on the new language and 30% for the language I know on an intermediate level." This allows her to build her languages in layers.

Judith uses a similar approach: "The approach that works best for me is to have just one beginner language that I'm actively studying and one intermediate or advanced language that I'm also focusing on. With the intermediate/advanced languages I sometimes focus on more than one but not with the beginner languages. That has always turned into a disaster!"

Develop personas for each language: Once you have made progress in several languages, it can be hard to compartmentalise them, especially if they are similar.

Natasha Asghar, a London-based presenter for Zee TV, speaks three Indo-Aryan languages and three European languages – four of which she uses in her job on a daily basis. She tells us: "I learnt English, Hindi, Urdu and Punjabi at the same time and then went on to study French and German later on. One useful tip for new learners is to develop 'personas' for each language. This will help keep them separate in your head."

So, for French, your persona may be a whimsical waitress like Amélie who smiles and gesticulates a lot. For German, it may be a stern scientist who speaks in clipped tones. If you adopt their mannerisms, their tone of speaking and cadence of speech, it will help you keep the languages separate.

If you layer your languages following the 70/30 rule, it may also help to change your environment for each language and study them on different days.

Be systematic: If you are serious about learning multiple languages, consider logging the hours you spend on each one.

Judith tells us: "I'm impatient when I don't quickly see results, so I keep a log of when I study and how long I study. I use a spreadsheet for this because daily updates should take no time at all. My current major project is Hebrew and I can tell exactly that I have studied 136 hours of Hebrew since January 1st, which is a little over half an hour per day on average."

Recording your study in this way will encourage you to celebrate small wins, motivate you to keep putting in the hours and give you solid metrics against which to measure future language efforts.

Understand that language learning is more long than hard: Most of us believe that language learning is hard. Without a doubt, it can be frustrating, challenging and unrewarding for long stretches of time but it's not hard in the same way astrophysics or advanced mathematics are hard. Learning multiple languages – or indeed just one – is more *long* than hard. Even the arguably 'easy' languages take 600 hours of study to achieve proficiency.

Staying focused and motivated is clearly the key. San Francisco-based designer Shannon Del Vecchio speaks English, Spanish, Italian, Portuguese and Japanese. She tells us: "When I first met my wife, Gina, I already spoke four languages. I learned Italian in part because her family is

111

Italian and I now have an Italian last name. She used to tell everyone, 'Shannon is so good at languages! She is amazing! She speaks four of them like it's nothing.' After watching me learn Italian, she now says, 'You would not believe Shannon's power of concentration when it comes to learning languages. She can sit down and work on it for two hours and nothing sways her focus. It is crazy.'

Don't worry about keeping them all in your head: One concern about learning, say, French may be that it will somehow 'override' your progress in Spanish, but your brain has space for both.

Academic Nayr Ibrahim writes: "The separate underlying proficiency (SUP) hypothesis theory, now discredited, suggests that languages are stored in separate compartments or containers, which represent half the capacity of the monolingual brain. These 'containers' have limited storage space, and, as the brain cannot hold so much information, it 'elbows out' the other language … Decades of research into bi- and multilingualism has shown that there is no causal relationship between bilingualism and language delay."

Don't be defeated by the fear of losing a language before you even begin.

CHAPTER 13: SAFETY & SECURITY

84. Check government advice

We have been to a number of destinations in times of unrest, from Egypt in 2012 right after the Arab Spring to Turkey in 2016 in the midst of a number of bombings. We have never encountered danger first hand but perhaps this was more luck than sense.

Our advice to travellers is to check government warnings and follow relevant advice in making a decision.

- UK: gov.uk/foreign-travel-advice
- US: travel.state.gov/content/travel/en.html
- Australia: dfat.gov.au/travel/Pages/travel.aspx
- Canada: travel.gc.ca

Of course, risk is a highly personal choice. Our ethos is 'travel with abandon' and if there is any solid guiding principle we can offer, it would have to be that. As independent travellers, we would urge our peers to explore as much as their nerve would allow. If we had shied away from Turkey, we would never have seen some of the most unique landscapes in 60 countries of travel.

Perhaps extreme climber Jimmy Chin explains it best: "The two great risks are risking too much but also risking too little. That's for each person to decide. For me, not risking anything is worse than death."

85. Don't neglect basic safety

When months of travel pass without incident, it's natural to become complacent; to stop using the hotel safe, to stop diligently splitting your money, to ignore the fact that the bike you hired doesn't come with a helmet. I (Kia) have learnt the hard way that complacency leads to trouble, from having my bag snatched in Colombia to falling off my bike (sans helmet) in Cambodia. Follow the basics at all times.

Protect yourself

- Buy a personal alarm
- Check in with friends regularly
- Always insist on a helmet
- Always use a seatbelt where available
- Follow local customs in terms of dress
- Watch your drinking
- Get travel insurance
- Keep copies of your documentation (see tip 16. Carry photocopies)
- Check reviews

Protect your stuff

- Always pack valuables in your hand luggage
- Slip your daypack's strap around your leg at restaurants and bus stations
- Make use of the hotel safe
- Don't use wire mesh; they're not that safe and signal that you have valuables worth stealing
- Install Find My iPhone (or equivalent app) to track your phone
- Consider a portable safe (pacsafe.com)
- And, of course, don't offer papaya!

86. Avoid common scams

Tourists are prime targets for scam artists so it's useful to understand their most common tactics as detailed below.

Credit card scam: This includes anything from cloning your card to swiping it twice. A standard scam involves a store owner who takes your card to swipe it and then swipes it again at a higher price and/or forges your signature. Don't let your credit card out of your sight.

Hotel scam: You arrive at a new destination and hail a taxi only to be told your pre-booked hotel is fully booked, has now closed down or burnt to the ground. Instead, you're taken to another hotel and the taxi driver takes a commission. If this happens, insist on being taken to your requested hotel. If the driver won't honour your request, get another taxi.

If you have prepaid for your hotel (online or at check-in), keep the receipt. This prevents dishonest hoteliers from demanding a second payment on checkout.

Taxi scam: Always agree prices or insist on a meter before you take a taxi. On occasion, drivers may tell you "not to worry" or "we'll sort it out later" and then demand ridiculous tariffs. Another trick is when the driver drives off with your luggage after receiving the fare. Our advice is to pay only after you've retrieved your cases. You can also leave the door open while you get the luggage from the trunk.

Money-changing scam: There is a whole host of money-changing scams, from issuing fake or discontinued bank notes to simply slipping notes up a sleeve. The safest and easiest way to avoid money-changing scams is to use recommended dealers, watch your money extra carefully and double-check the amount in front of the teller before you leave.

Fake police scam: It's not unusual for fake police officers to approach tourists, quickly flash a fake badge and request to see documents or issue a fine for some unforeseen encroachment. Always insist on seeing ID again and inspect it properly. You can make a show of noting down his or her name, an ID number and any other information. You can also ask to accompany him or her to a police station or ask a local to step in for help. Usually a crook will want to avoid a public scene and give up.

Train station scam: During my last trip to India, a very official looking man approached me (Peter) and said that my train had been cancelled and that I should go with him to buy a ticket for an alternative route. I followed and checked the departures board en route to find that my train was still on there. After a short argument, the man gave up and I spotted him later trying the same thing on another unsuspecting tourist. It's good practice to check word-of-mouth updates with an official behind a desk.

Pickpocketing scam: Somebody spills something on you or distracts you while someone else lifts items from your pockets. There are reports of young children pestering tourists or even a mother handing over a baby while someone else pickpockets an unaware victim.

Drug trafficking scam: You may become an unwitting drug mule if someone slips something into your luggage or asks you for help in delivering a package, carrying a bag, or pushing a pram across a border. Never lose sight of your luggage and never ever agree to carry something for a stranger.

Common sense: There are numerous variants of these scams and the advice is nearly always the same: keep your possessions, credit cards and documents in sight; challenge suspicious behaviour; insist on receipts and identification;

always remain vigilant. This is particularly applicable in crowded areas like bus and train stations and major tourist attractions.

87. How to deal with street harassment

Travelling as a lone female is generally safe as long as you know how to handle yourself. Firstly, read tip 85. Don't neglect basic safety. In terms of street harassment in particular:

- Dress like the local women.
- Consider wearing a fake wedding ring.
- Walk with confidence.
- Research local conduct. In some countries, it's acceptable to engage with the instigator and politely say no; in others, you shouldn't make eye contact at all. In others still, it's advised that you shout the local words for 'honour' or 'shame' to embarrass the man into skulking away. Research is key.
- If you feel threatened, retrieve your personal alarm.
- If you get followed, go to a busy shop and ask the owner for help.
- If the harasser gets physical, trigger your alarm or start screaming. Pleading or negotiating is generally not effective.
- If the assailant is in a car or van, run the opposite way as it's harder for them to turn around.
- Fight back: Aim for the knees, privates and eyes.

88. What to do in an emergency

Stay calm: Robert Frost once wrote, "In three words I can sum up everything I've learned about life: it goes on" – and it's true. It may feel like the world is ending, but things will be okay.

Ask for help: Most locals will be happy to help, even if you don't speak the language. Ask for help in getting to a police station or getting online.

File a police report: Go to the police station nearest to where the robbery occurred, report the robbery and ask for a numbered copy of the police report. You can ask a local to point the way there. It may feel like a waste of time as the police will likely do nothing to retrieve your bag, but the report will help in ordering a replacement passport and processing your insurance claim.

Visit your embassy: Present your police report at your embassy. This will expedite your passport. If the embassy is closed, visit first thing in the morning. If the queue is long, it's worth asking someone if you have the right line.

Call your insurance company: You may need to reverse charges by dialling the international operator on 155 (not available on mobile). Good insurers will accept reverse charges and keep you on the line while they cancel your credit cards and have new ones issued. We use World Nomads (worldnomads.com).

Cancel your bank cards: If the insurer hasn't done this, do it yourself. Hopefully, you have saved the contact details in your password sheet as discussed in tip 18. Create a password sheet.

Cancel your phone line: Report your phone as lost or stolen. Hopefully, you have saved the contact details in your password sheet as discussed in tip 18. Create a password sheet.

Get emergency cash: If your insurer doesn't supply you with emergency cash, contact Western Union if you have someone at home that can send you money (UK 0800 833 833; USA 1800 325 6000, westernunion.com). You will have to pay a fee. If you don't have ID, you can pick up the money using a code word – *very* 007.

89. Download TripWhistle

When we set off on our first trip around the world, we put Vanuatu's emergency numbers for police, fire and medical in our phones along with our travel insurance policy numbers and contact details for the British embassy.

As our trip progressed, we became increasingly complacent to the point where we had no idea what the emergency numbers were during our visit to Colombia (one of the most violent countries in the world).

We've since discovered TripWhistle (itunes.com), a comprehensive list of emergency numbers across the world. It allows you to make a call from within the app and displays your location while on the phone. It's the sort of app you don't know you need until you need it, so be safe and download it now.

90. When in Rome, don't be an idiot

If you're in a big party town, go ahead and go crazy. If you're at a peaceful retreat, then try your hand at pretentious Pilates. There's nothing wrong with getting into the spirit of a place, but don't be stupid about it.

In 2008, a few years before I met Peter, I was on the beach in Miami when a green-eyed model specimen of a man approached me. After a short conversation, he asked if I wanted to go for a swim. My British reserve mixed with my Asian conservatism (and the fact that I just felt a bit pale and flabby next to him) prompted me to decline. I've never done the casual thing so I denied his gentle attempts to persuade me.

Eventually, he looked at me with admonishment and said, "Come on! You're in Miami!" Those words triggered something in me. He was right. I was in Miami for Christ's sake. I had just come out of a messy relationship and though I wasn't about to *start* doing the casual thing, if I couldn't go for a swim with a model type in Miami, then I was too square to even be there. And thus with a warning that it would be 'just a swim' I stepped out of my dress and waded into the warm water with him.

A few minutes in, he began to get tactile and almost immediately I froze up. Gentle persuasion quickly turned into forcefulness and with his arms locked around me, I began to panic.

"Relax," he kept telling me. "Just relax." I tried to push him away to no avail. My protests grew increasingly panicked until, eventually, I spotted someone walking towards us. I told him in no uncertain terms to "let me go or I'll scream," which had the desired effect. I ran out of the water, gathered up my things and rushed back to the hotel.

I don't think I felt truly threatened while in the water; it was only when I was back safely that I realised how shaken I was. I realised how wrong things could have gone if I had made that snap decision in a slightly different place at a slightly different time. I'm by no means saying that anyone who makes a similar decision is an 'idiot'; it's just a way of saying *be careful.* Yes, travelling is about releasing inhibitions and having fun, but keep your wits about you and don't do something you'll regret.

CHAPTER 14: WORKING ON THE ROAD

91. Find remote work

More and more travellers are adopting remote work as a way to fund their travel lifestyles. If you want to do the same, there are several paths you can follow.

Continue your old role on a remote basis: If you work in a role that can be performed on a remote basis, consider talking to your manager about remote work. Most traditional companies won't agree to this, but there *is* a small chance. Consider if this is the route you want to take. If you're beholden to specific hours at your desk, you may find it stressful to fit work around travel schedules and sketchy wifi.

Freelance role: If you have a specific skill (writing, photographing, coding), consider setting up a freelance business. This is a good option as it has inbuilt flexibility. You can set your own hours and working patterns. though it may involve a lot of pitching, researching and chasing.

Find a new full-time role: The founders of Basecamp have made remote work a core part of their ethos. They run weworkremotely.com which is a great source for finding a range of fully remote positions. It has an emphasis on tech, but does include roles in business and marketing too.

92. Teach English as a foreign language

If English is your first language and you have a university degree, then teaching English as a foreign language is a great way to top up your travel allowance. In some cases, those two traits alone will be sufficient in securing some work but it will likely be low paid and on a casual basis (which may suit your needs just fine).

If you're serious about making some real money while travelling, it's better to get qualified before you leave home. There are several options available. The TEFL (Teaching English as a Foreign Language, tefl.co.uk), CELTA (Certificate in Teaching English to Speakers of Other Languages, cambridgeenglish.org) and TESOL (Teachers of English to Speakers of Other Languages, tesol.org) qualifications are all good options, recognised globally.

With one of these qualifications under your belt, you'll find it easier to find jobs, beat the unqualified competition and find it less daunting when stepping into the classroom for your first day of teaching.

Naturally, these courses don't come for free and you'll have to decide how serious you are about teaching English and whether it's worth the cost of the course. Generally, they come in at around $1,500 to $3,000 for an extended course spread over several weeks and about $350 for a weekend introductory course.

The pay varies depending on the school, company and class sizes. Bear in mind that roles may require a six- to 12-month contract.

Try:
- Teaching English: teachingenglish.org.uk
- ESL Cafe: eslcafe.com
- TEFL International: teflinternational.com
- ESL Base: eslbase.com

93. Volunteer

'Voluntourism' has come under much fire over the past few years, especially after a forthright piece by former voluntourist Pippa Biddle went viral (pippabiddle.com). In it, she urges would-be volunteers to consider whether or not they really possess the necessary skillset to make their trip worthwhile.

If you can indeed bring genuine value to a local community, then consider booking a project through an ethical volunteering organisation.

Try:
- GVI: gvi.co.uk
- Blue Ventures: blueventures.org
- Pod Volunteer: podvolunteer.org
- People and Places: travel-peopleandplaces.co.uk

94. Secure seasonal work

Seasonal jobs offer reasonably well-paid work even for those with little experience. Resort work, be it in winter or summer, is a good option.

Summer roles might include working as a counsellor at a kids' camp, bartending, waiting, receptionist work, housekeeping, cooking, supply driving, cleaning, guiding, sports instruction, working as a lifeguard, scuba instruction and more.

Winter resort work will likely include much of the above as well as more specific roles such as a ski tuner, lift operator, snowmobile guide, ski guide, ski rental shop clerk and chalet cleaner. Be aware that ski and winter sports resorts often require applications in writing beforehand.

Some of the most common seasonal jobs for travellers can be found during the harvest seasons. Think fruit gathering in Australia or grape picking in France. Pay is usually based on what you can pick in a day so it may take a while to get up to speed but the chances are you'll be working with people in the same boat as you.

There are also exchange opportunities available where you can volunteer in exchange for food and board. This bypasses the need for a work permit as you will not be legally employed.

Try:
- HelpX: helpx.net
- InterExchange: interexchange.org
- WWOOF-ing: wwoof.org.uk

95. Crew a yacht

Yachties are often looking for crew, offering an excellent opportunity to travel relatively cheaply albeit slowly with some seasickness thrown in for good measure.

It's not all hard work though. A lot of the time, crewmembers will only be expected to take a turn on watch: scanning the horizon for cargo ships, stray shipping containers (UFOs: unidentified floating objects) and the occasional reef. Other jobs may include cleaning, cooking and general upkeep of the boat.

In port, there may be other jobs available such as diving and scraping of the hull, painting and making repairs, and preparing the boat for the next voyage.

Often, sailing experience isn't necessary but whatever you have will go a long way when negotiating your berth. I (Peter) have a couple of dinghy qualifications which help with terminology but in general crew members can learn as they go. Most yachties charge crew from $25 per day for food and provisions.

If you're trying to find a berth on a yacht, check noticeboards at marinas, enquire at yacht clubs and moorings, and check out the following sites.

- Crewseekers: crewseekers.net
- Crewbay: crewbay.com
- Findacrew: findacrew.net

As a general rule, about 3m of length (of the yacht) for each crew member reflects relatively comfortable conditions. It's worth noting that yachts are considerably more comfortable if they have a dodger to protect the helmsman to and keep out the weather, a furling jib, as well as an onboard shower and toilet. Yachts rigged for ocean racing are generally more workable than recreational liveaboards.

Just remember that ocean-going boats can be dangerous, conditions can change in a heartbeat and seasickness can ruin a trip. Saying that, the rewards of sailing are incomparable and offer a beautiful and unrivalled view of the world. The best advice is to try and crew a small trip before you sign up for a multi-week crossing of the Pacific!

96. Start a travel blog

Yes, we know: it seems that every man and his dog now has a travel blog but starting your own is a great way to share your travels and can keep you attuned to the demands of work. A professional blog shows that you can think creatively and work diligently. It showcases your writing and photography skills (if indeed you have them!) and shows that you have a wealth of employable skills: marketing, social media management, search engine optimisation, business development, product management and so on.

We recommend WordPress and Bluehost (bluehost.com) to get started. See our post on how to start a travel blog (atlasandboots.com/how-to-start-a-travel-blog) for a comprehensive step-by-step guide to setting up your site, but here's an overview so you know what's involved.

- Choose your brand name
- Register your domain
- Set up hosting
- Install WordPress
- Install a theme
- Install core tools and plugins
- Prepare an editorial calendar
- Create a pro-forma to record details
- Invest in good photography
- Write well and read, read, read
- Actively promote your posts and blog

CHAPTER 15: COMING HOME

97. Stay employable

Our trip around the world was the best decision we ever made but it didn't come without concerns. We knew we wanted a slower pace of life but also that we would have to find jobs once we returned to London.

The fear of ruining a carefully built career has put many people off travelling. In some fields, the fear is warranted (for example, most junior doctors can't leave their jobs for a year) but for most of the rest of us, a long-term trip is perfectly possible especially if we spend time on the road cultivating employable skills. Here's how.

Go somewhere different: There's nothing wrong with going to Thailand or India but going somewhere truly different will demonstrate a number of employable skills: problem solving, confidence, courage, curiosity and originality. Why not try Bhutan or Bangladesh instead?

Take on freelance work: If you have a specific skill that can be offered remotely (e.g. writing, video-editing, web development), consider taking on some freelance contracts. This not only provides supplemental income but also demonstrates that you can prioritise tasks, meet deadlines and work with people in a professional context.
Learn a language: Ah, yes. This old chestnut. So many of us have 'learn a language' on our bucket lists but few manage to tick it off. If you combine travel with language learning

and practice, you will demonstrate dedication and discipline – two highly employable skills.

It's unlikely you will become fluent in a year and most jobs won't actually use your language skills but it's not the language itself that's impressive; it's the time and effort you put into it as well as your willingness to learn. If you can pause at a language school and complete a certified course, then even better.

Take on a physical challenge: If you enjoy the outdoors, consider taking on an impressive physical challenge on your travels. This will demonstrate tenacity, determination and resourcefulness – all highly employable skills.

Perhaps you can climb Aconcagua on your trip through South America (the highest peak on the continent and one of the seven summits) or, on an even grander scale, cycle from Cape to Cairo. Achieving something substantial will provide a tangible reason for your travels and is more likely to win over potential employers in the future.

Run a website: See tip 96. Start a travel blog.

Volunteer: See tip 93. Volunteer.

98. Don't fear the frugal life

As the daughter of a Bangladeshi immigrant, I (Kia) have always been conscious of money – not enough to chase it but enough to ensure that I always have a buffer. I never had a credit card before our trip (and the one I took out for emergencies sits dusty and unused), I paid off my student loan before I had to, I always paid my bills as soon as they came in and was generally super-responsible with money – until our return.

We returned to London and for the first time in my adult life, I found myself with zero savings. This would have freaked me out a year or two ago but, today, I'm okay with it.

Our year of travel was worth it. We wouldn't live without a buffer all the time, but what's the point of savings if you don't use them on something great once in a while?

99. How to cope with city life

As our first trip around the world entered its final month, I (Kia) found my nerves jangling at the thought of returning to London.

Ask me to describe a scenario typical to, say, Samoa and I would tell you how Samoans constantly swap seats and rearrange themselves on buses to make sure as many people as possible have a seat, usually even offering their own laps.

Ask me a similar question of London and I'd probably tell you about the time I watched a man trip down the stairs at Oxford Circus tube station. He tumbled forward and landed upside down, head on the floor, legs splayed across the stairs. He had a glazed look in his eyes and had lost a shoe in the process. Everyone around me froze for a second, trying to decide if he was clumsy or drunk, wondering if they should help him or ignore him. We all opted for the latter, carefully picking our way around him.

As I passed, I heard him say "Sorry", his voice lucid and embarrassed. In that moment I hated myself for not trying to help or reassure him. Big cities numb you to other people: their problems, their pains, their very presence. Perhaps it's necessary as a survival tactic. Perhaps it's just not possible to care about eight million people when you're all jostling for space in a suffocating city, but there *are* small things we can do to make life easier for us and those around us.

Stop fighting for fragments of time: There's a special kind of anger that bubbles inside me when I'm stuck behind a person that treats rush hour like a Sunday stroll – and does so right in the middle of the stairwell. Sometimes I'm angry because I need to get where I'm going. Other times it's simply out of habit. Of course, rushing around gains us only tiny fragments of time: seconds, maybe minutes if we're lucky. Think about all the time you spend in boring meetings or in front of the TV or on Facebook. No one likes a long commute but how about giving up five minutes of Facebook instead of mowing people down to claw back some time?

Be conscious of other people's space: That means legs and elbows in the boundaries of your seat. That means not shoving your newspaper or phone or Kindle right in someone's face. It means not leaning on a pole that's meant for people to hold on to. It means not pushing the person in front of you when getting on a train – or trying to board before everyone's got off. It means moving down the aisle. It means picking up your litter. It means not blowing smoke into other people's faces. It means not shouting into your phone or playing your music too loud. It means not jumping the queue. It means being aware that people are around you.

Give your barista or newsagent or waitress your full attention: City life is super busy and I understand the need to multi-task but, really, phone calls should be made before you get to the head of a queue. When you talk to someone serving you, have the decency to put away your phone. Look them in the eye and talk to them. They are not part of a faceless mass that simply does your bidding. They are not the invisible fabric that holds together our cities. They are human beings and they deserve our attention.

Say thank you: It was Peter that first opened my eyes to how rude Londoners can be. He comes from a small town where people say thank you if you stop to let them pass in a supermarket aisle, or hold a door open for them – which of course means that big cities drive him crazy. As a native Londoner, I didn't even notice this behaviour until it was expressly pointed out to me. And now I notice it all the time. A thank you costs nothing so next time someone does you a courtesy, offer one back.

Take a flyer: Come on, we all know that handing out flyers in the freezing cold must be a soul-crushing endeavour. Just take what's offered to you, smile and say thank you. Take it and read it, or take it and recycle it, or take it and bin it. Just make someone's life a little bit easier that day.

Always carry headphones: Sometimes, your regard for others will not be reflected back to you. One of the most effective ways to stop yourself hating people is to have your headphones and music at arm's reach. This may not be actively making your city a better place, but it will make it more bearable for you.

Don't make assumptions about people: You know that girl in the head-to-toe burka? Do you see the Louboutins underneath her shapeless black cloak or the piercing in her left nipple? What about the guy with the cravat? Must be a city wanker, right? Well, actually, he was in the Peace Corps and works at a homeless shelter once a fortnight — he's just dressed up for a funeral. Big cities are full of archetypes but that doesn't mean people are shapeless blobs of predetermined characteristics. I've learnt – partly through surprising experiences and partly through tough lessons – not to label people because of the way they look or the name they sport. We'd all feel better about those around us if we saw them as individuals instead of representations.

Finally… if someone falls over, ask if they're okay: It's just not acceptable to step over someone and go on your merry way. If someone takes a tumble or very clearly needs some help, offer them your help. The Bystander Effect suggests that the more people present in a situation, the less likely they are to help because they assume someone else will. Be that person.

100. Travelling won't get travelling out of your system

Our big trip was meant to be our **big trip**, our one long adventure before we returned to normal life. Alas, we haven't rid ourselves of the travel bug. If anything, it's made us even more keen to visit places we haven't yet seen: Asia Minor, most of Africa, Greenland, Canada, Antarctica and more. There's a world out there and we have seen only a slice.

Don't expect travelling to beat travelling from your system.

APPENDIX A: PACKING LIST

This section provides a comprehensive packing list. Not everything is essential and you may wish to pick and choose items according to your interests and habits.

To avoid redundancy, each item appears only once even if it falls into two categories. For example, 'Laptop' is listed under 'Daypack' but not in 'Electronics'. Similarly, 'Hiking boots' is listed under 'Clothing & Shoes' and not 'Outdoor'. As such, make sure you read the entire list.

It's also worth noting that the items listed in 'Daypack' pertain to actual travel time (i.e. taking flights or long bus journeys). For days out sightseeing, you should leave your important documents in the hotel safe and carry photocopies instead.

Finally, the starred items (*) indicate the 10 outdoor essentials you should pack on hikes, treks and expeditions.

Daypack

Passport
Documentation (ID, travel insurance, visas, jabs list, onward tickets, photocopies)
Laptop
Phone
Camera
Kindle
Headphones
Water bottle
Earplugs and eye mask
Toothpaste and toothbrush
Neck pillow
Sunglasses
Notebook and pen
Guidebook
Personal alarm

Clothing & footwear

Waterproof jacket
Fleece
2 lightweight shirts or blouses
3 lightweight t-shirts
2 vests or dresses
1 pair of waterproof trousers
1 pair of zip-off trousers
2 pairs of shorts
Hat
Buff or scarf
Gloves
1 pair of swimwear
7 pairs of underwear
4 pairs of socks
Walking boots
Trainers or sports sandals
Flip-flops and/or ballet flats

Toiletries

Toothbrush and toothpaste
Shampoo
Soap
Razors and/or epilator
Facewash
Moisturiser
Deodorant
Hairbrush or comb
Hairdryer (optional but useful!)
Sanitary products (tampons, towels or Mooncup)
Wet wipes
Hand sanitiser
Quick-dry towel

Health

Sunscreen*
Lifesystems Pocket First Aid*
Water purifier
Painkillers
Antihistamines (e.g. Cetirizine)
Diarrhea medication (e.g. Imodium)
Motion sickness medication (e.g. Stugeron)
Insect repellent
Birth control
Mosquito net

Outdoor

Map and compass*
Insulation (extra clothing)*
Torch*
Lighter*
Repair kit and tools*
Nutrition (extra food)*
Hydration (extra water)*
Emergency shelter*
Penknife
Sleeping bag
Sleeping mat
Whistle
Waterproof stuffsacs

*Part of the outdoor '10 essentials'

Electronics & photography

Chargers for all gadgets (see gadgets in 'Daypack')
Global power adaptor (e.g. OREI adaptor)
Solar power charger (e.g. MSC solar chargers)
Tough cam
DSLR body
Lenses (wide angle, zoom)
Filters (ND and polarizing)
Tripod
Gorillapod (mini-tripod)
Extra batteries
Memory cards (large capacity)
External hard drive for storage
Camera bag or case

APPENDIX B: APPS & SITES

Plan

TripAdvisor: tripadvisor.com
Google Maps: maps.google.com
Lonely Planet: lonelyplanet.com
Wikivoyage: wikivoyage.org
Seat61: seat61.com
Busbud: busbud.com

Book

Skyscanner: skyscanner.net
Booking.com: Booking.com
Airbnb: airbnb.com
Hostelworld: hostelworld.com
Trusted Housesitters: trustedhousesitters.com
AirTreks: airtreks.com
SeatGuru: seatguru.com
Pitchup: pitchup.com

On the road

XE: xe.com
Western Union: westernunion.com
Onavo: onavo.com
Foodspotting: foodspotting.com
Hitchwiki: hitchwiki.org
WebFlyer: webflyer.com
FlightStats: flightstats.com
InterNations: internations.org

Work

Crewbay: crewbay.com
Crewseekers: crewseekers.net
Find a Crew: findacrew.net
WWOOF: wwoof.org.uk
HelpX: helpx.net
InterExchange: interexchange.org
GVI: gvi.co.uk
Blue Ventures: blueventures.org
Pod Volunteer: podvolunteer.org
Travel People and Places: travel-peopleandplaces.co.uk

Safety

TripWhistle Global SOS: itunes.com
First Aid by Red Cross: redcross.org
SnakeBite911: crofab.com/snakebite911
Cairn: cairnme.com

Language

Duolingo: duolingo.com
Diigo: diigo.com
Google Translate: translate.google.com
Quizlet: quizlet.com
Rosetta Stone: rosettastone.co.uk
TuneIn: tunein.com
Yabla: yabla.com
Italki: italki.com

DISCLAIMER:

The publishers and authors have done their best to ensure the accuracy and currency of all the information in **Don't Offer Papaya: 101 Tips for Your First Time Around the World**. However, they cannot accept any responsibility for loss, injury, or inconvenience sustained by any person as a result of information or advice contained in the book.

Atlas & Boots
atlasandboots.com

Instagram: instagram.com/atlasandboots
Twitter: twitter.com/atlasandboots
Facebook: facebook.com/atlasandboots
YouTube: youtube.com/atlasandboots